What early readers are say
Ten Powerful Things to Say t

"This should be required reading for every teacher."
—Kathy Rades, retired teacher, Lakewood, WA

"This was the best investment of two hours and
the best parenting book that I have ever read."
—Stacy Cahalan, Overland, KS

"Reading this book has made me more attuned to parent-child
conversations and relationships in general. It's also helping me
with my boys, even though they are in college."
—Don Gallagher, Olathe, KS

"A focused, honest book guaranteed to enhance your awareness of how
you communicate with your children. The author provides enlightened
ways to deepen your connections. Don't delay reading this one!"
—Mary Halbleib, Corvallis, OR

"This book raises awareness, which creates the opportunity
to be more purposeful and intentional about our relationships
with our children. A wonderful read!"
—Robert Boyle, Milan, IL

"Paul Axtell has put together a book that says exactly what
I believe parents need to know in order to raise children who feel
confident and competent, as children, teens, and adults.
A clear, concise, and inspirational read!"
—Bev Larson, PhD, Founder of Old Mill Center
for Children and Families, Corvallis, OR

JACKSON
CREEK PRESS

Ten
Powerful
Things
to Say
to
Your
Kids

*Creating the relationship you want with
the most important people in your life*

Paul Axtell

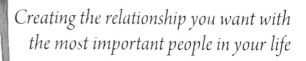

JACKSON CREEK PRESS

Illustrations by Jane Elizabeth Barr

Design by Cheryl McLean

Author photo by Cindy Officer

JACKSON CREEK PRESS

2150 Northwest Jackson Creek Drive

Corvallis, Oregon 97330

jacksoncreekpress.com

tenpowerfulthingstosay.com

ISBN 978-0-943097-09-1

Library of Congress Control Number: 2011935968

Printed in the USA

For

Haley

Collin

Adam

Camille

Trey

Isabel

Gabrielle

Reece

Ben

Sam

Zoe

Caroline

and

Abigail

We do not believe in ourselves until someone reveals that deep inside us, something is valuable, worth listening to, worthy of our trust, sacred to our touch. Once we believe in ourselves, we can risk curiosity, wonder, spontaneous delight, or any experience that reveals human spirit.

—e. e. cummings, poet

Contents

Acknowledgments

First of all, I must thank Jesse and Amy for being wonderful kids and friends and being willing to allow me to use them as examples in class. I can still remember Amy saying to me, "I bet this will end up in your teaching!" I also want to acknowledge their mother, Rebekah, for her importance in their lives.

This book would not have happened if Gwil Evans, who has taught me more than I ever thought I would know about writing, had not introduced me to Cheryl, my editor, who made it happen.

From an idea point of view, I owe a lot to Tim Gallwey, Michael Nichols, Dale Carnegie, and countless other authors and teachers who contributed to my thinking on what it means to be effective. You will find their teaching reflected throughout this book.

I owe a special thank you to all the parents who attended my classes and were willing to share their concerns and stories about raising their children.

And, like Pooh and Piglet *(page 28)* and everyone else, I needed a person walking beside me. Cindy, you are wonderful.

Early drafts of the manuscript were significantly improved through the advice and counsel of Elle Allison, Ranee Axtell, Cheri Boline, Bob Boyle, Sheila Burns, Stacy Cahalan, Nate Clark, Bill Cook, Reeny Davison, Moira Dempsey, Jessica DuPont, Phil Eckman, Gwil Evans, Lori Fanello, Amy Fettig, Don Gallagher, Paul Garcia, Lori Glander, Mary Halbleib, Bill and Sue Hall, Peg Herring, Bob and Donna Hughes, Liz James, Bev Larson, Missy MacInnis, Megan McClelland, Beverly McFarland, Anne Mitchell, Dana and Scott Nygaard, Pat Newport, Mark Oehler, Cathy Pinter, Kathy Rades, Sabah Randhawa, Lynda Rands, Jim Regan, Beverly Rutledge, Jennifer Schmidt, Sally Goetz Shuler, Keith and Kathleen Smith, Alice Sperling, Haley Stafford, Melissa Thomas, and Marilyn Trefz. I am indebted to each of them.

A special thanks also to Ellis, Chelsea, Zoe, Ben, Jared, Caroline, Jessica, Cassidy, Keegan, Aidan, Anni, David, Trey, and Adam, and to those parents, friends, and colleagues who shared their stories with us. You help keep it real.

Preface

I began thinking about this book a long time ago when I encountered a list of the most common things parents said to their kids. As you can imagine, the list was fairly negative, beginning with the number one statement, which was *No.*

A couple of other phrases on the list also hit home: *Why can't you be more like your brother? How many times do I have to tell you?*

My own children, Jesse and Amy, were nine and eight years old at the time, and the list prompted me to become more conscious of what I was saying to them directly—and what I was saying in their presence.

Then recently I read the book *Talent Is Overrated* by Geoff Colvin. One of the points the author makes is that you should tell your kids they are fast learners. Wow, I thought. That is so obvious and yet so profound.

That idea brought me back to writing this book. Jesse and Amy are now in their thirties, and I have thirteen wonderful grandchildren in the combined families with my wife, Cindy, and her three children—so there is still a place for us to be mindful about what we say.

For the past twenty-five years, I've worked as a coach and trainer focused on individual and group effectiveness. Within that focus, a central point is treating conversation as though it really matters. For me, there is a parallel between being effective at work and being effective as a parent. That parallel is conversation.

When I work with organizations on the value of conversation, I often use families as an analogy for communicating ideas about the relationships people have at work. Most parents in the group begin thinking about the conversations they have—or don't have—with their children. And this is true whether I'm working with engineers in Iowa or managers in Brazil, secretaries in Ohio or university deans in Oregon. The concerns and insights these parents shared as we talked about effective conversations— at work and at home—both added to my incentive for writing this book and contributed to the thinking behind it.

So now I'm turning those analogies around, using the lessons learned in teaching adults to communicate effectively at work to show you how these ideas can help you build more meaningful relationships at home. I hope you will see this as a powerful opportunity to transform your conversations—and your relationships—with your kids.

The Original List

What kids hear us say

Twenty-some years ago, a class participant brought me a list ranking the thirty statements children hear most from adults. I've tried to find its origin to no avail, but it caught my attention and inspired me to write this book.

Some of these statements would change if the original authors were to redo the list now. For example, iPods and ear buds have probably eliminated complaints about loud radio, but today's list might include something about not texting friends at dinner or playing too much Nintendo Wii.

Still, the overall message remains relevant: **There is not much that's positive in this set of statements**. Take a look:

1. No! (The answer most often heard)
2. Don't give me those excuses!
3. Let me put it another way.
4. I don't have time now; maybe later.
5. Do you think I'm made out of money?
6. Just wait until you have kids of your own.
7. What in the world do you think you are doing?
8. Don't eat a snack; dinner is almost ready.

9. Be nice to your little sister (brother) or else!

10. Clean your room.

11. When I was your age…

12. Are you lying to me?

13. Eat your dinner; there are children starving all over the world.

14. Can't you understand what I'm trying to tell you?

15. Can't you ever do (get) anything right?

16. Who do you think you are, anyway?

17. Why don't you grow up?

18. This is going to hurt me more than it will hurt you.

19. When are you ever going to learn?

20. Do it now!

21. Can't you kids get along with each other?

22. Why can't you be more like_____?

23. Go to your room!

24. Do your homework!

25. Don't use that tone of voice with me!

26. Shut up and listen to me!

27. You're not old enough to understand that yet.

28. Here, let me show you how to do it right.

29. I'm doing this for your own good.

30. Turn that radio down (off)!

As this list indicates, negative comments often shape the conversations parents have with their kids. At first blush, you may be dismayed by how many of these statements you can remember saying to your own kids. That certainly doesn't mean there is something wrong with you or with how you're raising your children. My point is simply that there is profound benefit in becoming more aware of what you say to your kids. Awareness gives you the choice to say something else, and therein lies the power. Awareness creates the opportunity for different conversations—conversations that open the door to more special moments with your children.

Calvin: Sometimes when I'm talking, my words can't keep up with my thoughts. I wonder why we think faster than we speak.

Hobbes: Probably so we can think twice.

—Bill Watterson, creator of the
Calvin & Hobbes comic strip

Think before you speak.

Although everyone grows up knowing the basics of how to speak and listen, day-in and day-out many people simply don't think about their conversations—about what they say or how well they listen. And, like most things in life, when you stop thinking about what you are doing or saying, you lose your ability to be effective in the moment.

Simply noticing the negative comments in your conversations with your kids is a perfect way to start. If you start to observe your conversations, you'll begin to notice, and the minute you notice, you can decide to change. Yankees catcher Yogi Berra said, "You can observe a lot just by watching." That may seem simple, but it works.

As you start looking, ask yourself these five questions, and the answers will reveal ways you can start to improve the conversations you have with your kids.

- *First, what would your children say they hear from you most often?* What are the things you say or ask several times a week? Or, in the deeper sense, what are the conversations that shape your relationship?

- *Second, how do you respond to problems?* What are typical problems that come up in your family, and how do the conversations go when these situations occur? For example, if your son brings home a report card with all A's except for one B-minus, what will he hear? The typical reaction might be something like, *What are you going to do to get that B-minus up?* Or, if your daughter plays a wonderful soccer game, scores a goal, and helps her team win—but is out of position a couple of times—what will she hear?

- *Third, what do you* **want** *your children to learn from you?* What do you want them to learn about life and about how to deal with the world?

- *Fourth, what do you want your kids to think about themselves?* What qualities and characteristics do you want to reinforce?

- *Fifth, what do you want your kids to know about you?*
  Consider sharing more about yourself, your childhood,
  your memories, what matters to you, what you worry
  about. Share things about yourself throughout your children's lives so they know you as a person as well as a parent.

When you think before you speak, you actually have the opportunity to make a *conscious choice* about what you want your kids
to hear from you. When you reflect on the conversations that
you are either having or not having, you can decide to change
the pattern of conversations in your family. You have a chance to
start fresh and make what you say and how you say it much more
meaningful and effective.

Don't worry that children never listen to you;
worry that they are always watching you.
—Robert Fulghum, American author

Something to think about...
What do you remember hearing from
your parents?

Twenty years from now, what do you want
your kids to remember hearing from you?

What You Say Matters.

In my years of training people in communication skills and effective conversation, these ideas have remained consistent:

- Your words and conversations create your reality, your future, and your relationships.

- What you talk about—or don't talk about—defines your relationship.

There's a third idea we'll discuss in more depth later: Without expressing yourself, without listening and paying attention, there's no conversation—and you lose the ability to create special relationships.

Think for a moment how language impacts the way children view themselves and the world. Young children pay attention to almost everything you do. They mimic you. They listen to what you have to say. They take what you say as the truth: If you say something is so, then it is so.

For example, you might tell someone, right in front of your son, that he is having a shy moment. He internalizes *shy* as what is true for him and continues to keep silent when adults speak to him.

You might have heard a child express a limiting thought about herself, something like *Girls can't do that*. If she says it, she is thinking it. And if she continues to think it, life may turn out that way for her. Here's a possible response to such a statement: "Really? Tell me about that." Then put the first element of possibility into her mind by saying, "Well, I'm not sure. I'm thinking that girls can do that, if they really want to." This is why *The Little Engine That Could* is one of my favorite books.

Sometimes a lot can be said without using words at all. At Thanksgiving, Zoe, age three, was sitting next to Haley, age fifteen, at the table. Zoe is a wonderful eater, willing to try anything. As the dishes were passed around the table, they came to Haley, who passed them to me so I could help Zoe with her portions. When the broccoli reached Haley, she made a face and passed the bowl to me. I began to put some broccoli on Zoe's plate, but Zoe immediately made the same face and said, "No broccoli!" One facial expression, and there went broccoli, perhaps forever.

This short exchange—though nonverbal—points to why it's important to be conscious of what you say to your children. Haley's reaction created a future for Zoe—one without broccoli.

Going broccoli-less through life might not be a grand tragedy, but you get the idea. Language has the power to change lives.

Here are six reasons why language and conversations matter:

- Your view of the world is shaped by the language and conversations you experience.

- You make decisions about your possibilities, capabilities, and limitations early in life based on what is said to you or in your presence.

- For children, there is a strong connection between conversation and learning. Reading and conversing are key developmental tools.

- Interacting powerfully and effectively in the world requires speaking, listening, and social skills.

- Your relationships are shaped by the pattern of your conversations.

- If you can talk openly and meaningfully about what matters, your relationships will be able to survive the difficulties that inevitably arise.

Let's look at what each of these means with regard to children.

Your view of the world is shaped by language and conversation. Two examples highlight what I mean. The first illustrates that words can hurt because we all take things personally. My mother used to say this rhyme to me: "Sticks and stones may break your bones, but words will never hurt you." I don't remember what circumstances prompted her to say it, but the point is that the rhyme would have been created only if words *do* hurt.

A more accurate version might be: "Sticks and stones may break your bones, but words can do even more damage."

The second example comes from an adage: If you want to change your kids, change their playground and their friends. In other words, expose them to a different set of conversations. This adage points to the notion that a big part of your environment is created by the conversations in which you live and grow up. You probably know people who are so negative you don't really like to be around them, or someone whom you can never seem to satisfy, or people who always have to be right or have things their way. You also probably know people you love to be around, who make you feel safe, who have wonderful attitudes about life, who make you feel worthy, valued, and special. Who do you want to be when you are with your kids?

Your words have the power to hurt as well as to nurture. The pattern of your conversations creates an environment that can be healthy or detrimental. The primary conversations that surround your children are *your* conversations—both with them directly and with others while your children are present. And those are the conversations you have the power to change.

You make decisions about what is possible for yourself early in life. Most people can identify decisions they made about themselves based on what they were told or what was said in their presence. For me, it was about being shy. When guests arrived and were introduced, I wouldn't say anything. My mother, being supportive, would step in and cover for me. "Oh, just give him a little time; he's just shy." At my first grade teacher's conference with Ms. Jenner, the same exchange occurred. Ms. Jenner commented on my lack of participation in class, and my mother explained that I was just shy. When you are three or four, you begin to think of yourself in the ways that people describe you. Then you begin to act in a way that is consistent with those labels or words or stories. Shyness is a particularly limiting story. I'd love to do high school over—I'd have a date this time. And it was hard to contribute early on in my work career because I tended not to participate or speak.

This is a common issue. I was working with a group of university administrators on being effective in group settings. We were discussing the importance of being able and willing to express oneself. At that point, a senior manager shared that she didn't speak in groups unless called upon because, when she was a child, her father had repeatedly told her she was backward. So here was a successful manager who was still curtailing a part of her life based on what was said to her when she was growing up.

Perhaps you were told you were not athletic or not coordinated, and those words made you decide not to play sports or try certain things in life. Those words—those labels—had a power far beyond the moment in which they were uttered. And in the case of the manager whose father called her backward, having the label repeated as a pattern in childhood meant that it continues to have an impact more than forty years later.

Sometimes a seemingly benign comment may have unintended consequences. My friend Marilyn and I were at a restaurant with her wonderful grandson, Keegan, who is four. He tried to balance his ice cream cone on the edge of his tray, and it tipped over. Marilyn reacted with, "That wasn't a smart thing to do."

"I knew immediately it wasn't a good thing to say," she said later. We all know telling a child he is not smart has no value. Using the word in an indirect fashion isn't useful, either. Better to have said, "Oops!" or "That didn't work!" in a lighthearted way.

Words have power.

I received this from a friend when I asked about her stories:

"I remember my mom saying to my sisters and me, 'Who do you think you are?' Inevitably, I would reply, 'Nobody. I don't think I'm anybody.'

"Later, I had to take control of my own sense of self to overcome this belief, because if you think you're 'nobody,' you settle for very little, you allow yourself to be in diminishing relationships, and you don't expect good things to happen to you. I changed this for myself, but many people do not.

"On a more upbeat note, I remember saying to my youngest sister when she was very little, 'You really are a great observer.' Today she's a museum curator, and she says it has something to do with that comment I made to her when she was just a little kid."

My point is you might say something that seems harmless and even true. But it's still a label. It's a story you made up. Better not to comment than to risk creating a limiting story for the child to grow up believing about himself. If you can be more aware of what you say, you can choose your words more carefully.

I've been guilty of this kind of labeling myself. One day I became frustrated with my grandson Ben and told him he was selfish. Far better for me to have said something like "Ben, I'd like you to share more often." Or, "Ben, I'd like you to give Sam a chance to play." The word *selfish* doesn't even need to be said. Now if this is the only time Ben hears the word *selfish*, it's probably fine. If it's repeated and becomes a pattern, it could begin to determine how he thinks about himself.

Labels—*shy, backward, selfish, not athletic, uncoordinated*, and the like—are limiting. Such comments may or may not persist over time. It depends on how often they are repeated. It's best if you don't say them at all, but the limiting patterns are truly what you need to avoid. Even positive statements—*athletic, studious, pretty*—could be limiting if that's always the focus of conversation.

What were you told when you were a child, and what did you decide as a result?

> *If you treat an individual as he is, he will remain as he is.*
> *If you treat an individual as he could be,*
> *he will become the person he could be.*
> —Johann Wolfgang von Goethe, German writer

For children, there is a connection between conversation and learning. Susan Engel, a psychology lecturer and director of the teaching program at Williams College in Massachusetts, wrote in a *New York Times* article, "In order to design a curriculum that teaches what truly matters, educators should remember a basic precept of modern developmental science." She says the activities that help children develop a new skill don't always look like the new skill being developed. "For example," Engel explains, "saying the alphabet does not particularly help children learn to read. But having extended and complex conversations during toddlerhood does."

Having conversations with your kids early on sets them up for developing a whole host of skills they'll need to be successful later in life. A kindergarten teacher once told me she could tell which kids weren't listened to at home because those children were not able to speak as well as others. They didn't have enough practice at home with speaking and being heard in order to develop that critical skill.

Interacting effectively in the world requires conversational skills. People don't come into the world equipped with good conversational skills; these have to be learned. But without such capability, it's difficult to excel in life. And it's much too important to wait until your kids are school age to be sure they develop the ability to communicate effectively.

Cindy and I have been working with our grandchildren on conversational skills. We do so by reading with them and consciously having conversations with them. Over the years, one very simple indicator of their conversational skills has been whether they can order for themselves at a restaurant—especially if it requires a back-and-forth conversation with the waiter. As a parent or grandparent, it's tempting to jump in and help. Resist!

I realize now that I was too careful with my kids or underestimated what they might have been capable of if given the opportunity. There were plenty of times I could have asked them to handle things on their own. For instance, I recently read about a woman who sat down with her ten-year-old son before a doctor's visit and together they wrote out the list of questions he would ask of the doctor. I wish I had thought of that!

I always wanted my kids to be able to speak effectively with adults. Short answers like *Fine* or *Whatever* didn't work for me. But I didn't really notice it until I asked my son, Jesse, to stand in for one of the players in a weekly doubles tennis match. One of my friends went out of his way to make Jesse comfortable by trying to engage him in a conversation. The exchange went something like this:

DON: "How is your summer going, Jesse?"

JESSE: "Okay."

DON: "Playing much tennis?"

JESSE: "Yes."

DON: "Playing any tournaments?"

JESSE: "Yes."

DON: "How are you doing?"

JESSE: "Okay."

Don sensed Jesse wasn't interested in talking and backed off. It's true that Don's questions allowed for yes or no answers. Still, Jesse could have taken the opportunity to talk about his tennis. I decided to work with Jesse, pointing out that he needed to notice when people invited him to speak, and he needed to learn to speak on demand—in something more than monosyllables. He might eventually have become comfortable speaking to adults on his own, but I wanted to be sure it happened.

Your relationships are shaped by the pattern of your conversations. If I were to ask your teenagers to identify what they can expect to hear from you every week, they could tell me. And that pattern of conversations would most likely define their sense of their relationship with you.

For example, when my daughter, Amy, was about twelve, she sat in on one of my training programs. During a break she asked me about the idea we had discussed in class that you could think of any relationship as a series of conversations. This is something I first read about in Deborah Tannen's book *You Just Don't Understand*. A professor of linguistics at Georgetown University, Tannen wrote, "Each person's life is lived as a series of conversations." Relationships might be viewed through this lens as well. I had suggested in class that you could look back at the last several conversations you had with someone to determine whether the relationship is what you want it to be. On the break, Amy said to me, "Dad, I've been counting, and the last twelve conversations we've had have been about homework. And that's not much of a relationship!"

Kids are insightful.

If you ask them, even very young children will be able to tell you what you say to them most often. After reading an early version of this manuscript, my daughter-in-law, Ranee, asked her three-year-old what she heard Mommy say most. Caroline answered, "You say 'I love you' most."

Even now, if I reflect on the conversations that make up my relationships with the people in my life, I can often see where I need to change the patterns. For example, Jesse and I both love sports. Talking about sports is a wonderful common ground. Still, if we limit our conversation to that topic, our relationship will be far less than I want it to be.

If you can talk openly and meaningfully about what matters, your relationships will be special. The ability to talk about difficult issues is what distinguishes ordinary relationships from special relationships. Can you talk with your children about things that matter? It's easy to talk about sports and movies. It's easy to talk when report cards are full of good grades. It's easy to talk when you are feeling good about yourself and about the relationship. The question is, can you talk when it's not going well, when you are upset, or when you really don't want to?

Most people are raised to avoid conflict, and, as a result, they often lack the skills needed to make relationships special. What do you do when you have a disagreement? Leave it unexpressed and try to go on as though it never happened? Seethe and simmer until you explode? Or take the time and energy to have the uncomfortable conversation—expressing yourself and listening to the other side—and get to a place of agreement or mutual understanding? To create truly meaningful relationships, it's essential to be able to raise issues and discuss them until everyone is satisfied with the outcome.

When children are small, it's easier to demand they do what you want them to do. As children grow older, you realize your ability to control their behavior disappears. So the sooner you start talking your way through situations, the better. If you start early—almost before you think they can understand what you are saying—it sets the stage for being able to talk things through as they get older.

It's not just about the words you choose. It's about learning to communicate in a way that builds connections instead of walls.

In fact, this is part of Deborah Tannen's view of conversation: You are either communicating with each other in a way that creates relationship, or you are interacting in a way that dominates or erodes the relationship. Simply reflecting on your recent conversations and thinking about these ideas will make a difference. You'll begin to notice and adjust your tone of voice, how you say things, and perhaps even how you look when you are interacting with your kids. If you want to come across as supportive, you will.

You might be too young to remember *The Ed Sullivan Show*, but he once had a guest who balanced plates on top of poles and set them spinning—something like eight or nine plates all spinning at once. As long as he could run over to plates that were beginning to wobble and give them a spin, he could keep adding plates.

It's a good metaphor for life and relationships. We tend to think of our family relationships as always there, always fine—never needing attention. Perhaps if we found a way to remind ourselves that our most important relationships are like those spinning plates—they need some attention to keep spinning—then we would make time to read with the kids or ask them to talk to us about what matters or plan date nights with our partners. Different relationships need different kinds of attention. You know your family. You know what each person likes to do. You know what each might ask for. And if you aren't sure, just ask.

Probably the most important message here is that it's never too late. I work with adults in all lines of work all over the country, and I can tell you—they have transformed their relationships with their co-workers, their employees, their bosses, and, most essentially, their families. They learned to make different choices about what conversations to have with the people most important to them—and to treat each conversation as though it matters.

Something to think about...

Whom do you love to watch interact with your kids?

How would you describe yourself when you are around your kids?

What teachers say matters.

A proud parent in one of my coaching programs shared this message from his daughter about a moment when one of her students helped her remember why she became a teacher. It's reprinted here with her permission.

"I was reminded by a senior student who was retaking his 10th grade second semester English class why I am in this profession.

"I asked Jared five essay questions. The last question was, 'What advice/suggestions would you give me as an English teacher (favorite part of class/least favorite part of class; favorite unit we studied/least favorite unit we studied)?'

"Jared's response was as follows:

"'My advice to you, Mrs. McGuire, would be to teach the kids about life. You're amazing at it already. Teach them about crossroads and tough decisions. Let them find their individuality, and teach them how to learn and write and talk to adults. Prepare them for what life has to offer and how much the world needs them. Just how you taught me. Don't change anything. You are one of the best. I was truly thankful to have you there in my high school career. Thanks!'

"My favorite line has to be, 'Prepare them for what life has to offer *and how much the world needs them.*' Isn't that both humbling and awesome?!"

The New List

Having looked at why it's important to pay attention to what you say, now let's look at some new things to say—new, that is, as compared to the original list of what kids heard most from their parents twenty years ago. The primary objective of this book is to encourage you to think about your conversations with your children in new ways. One of these is: *What do you want them to remember hearing you say?*

The next ten chapters of the book look more deeply at my top ten answers to that question:

1. **I like you.** This is a different statement from *I love you.* This statement says, *I like who you are as a person.* Use them both.

2. **You're a fast learner**. Learning is natural. Young children are amazing at it. Learning is play to them. What you say to them early influences how they relate to learning later in life, when it can be more difficult or frustrating.

3. **Thank you**. Simple courtesies are a sign of respect. Social skills are critical in life, and the best training for tact and grace starts early.

4. **How about we agree to...** This is about establishing a few basic agreements that set the stage for how you work together within the family. Having agreements in place

helps avoid common issues and provides a framework within which to solve problems when they do arise.

5. **Tell me more**. This is a request for your children to share their thoughts and feelings and ideas with you. It also involves learning to listen, which is always a gift because it signals that you care.

6. **Let's read**. Reading to your kids brings so many benefits. It helps them build skills they need for success in life. It enriches your relationship and instills a love of learning. And books provide a gateway to the world—people, places, and ideas. If you think about it, reading and interacting with your kids about a book is one of the earliest conversations you have with them.

7. **We all make mistakes**. Problems happen. No one is perfect. Dealing with problems and learning from mistakes are vital life skills. When you have a moment in which you don't live up to your own standards, it's an opportunity to show your children how to take responsibility for mistakes and move on. Kids can beat themselves up over not meeting your expectations or not being perfect. Giving each other a little room around this is a gift for both of you.

8. **I'm sorry**. It's something you can learn to say. This might not be an issue for you. It was for me, so it makes my list. Learning to catch yourself before saying what might later require an apology is an even more valuable skill.

9. **What do you think?** Asking for input and giving kids a chance to be part of family conversations lets them learn to exercise their decision-making skills and begin to take

responsibility for their choices. Expressing what you think and asking for what you want are fundamental skills that will serve your children throughout their lives.

10. **Yes**. While I do think *no* is still a viable option at times, too often parents are "a *no* waiting to happen." If you create a pattern of *yes* in your family, you'll find that *no* doesn't need to be said as often as you think.

The ten statements in this new list were absent in the original list. If you add them to your family conversations, I believe they will make a powerful difference in the relationship you can have with your kids—and to the way your children will begin to see themselves in the world. My hope is that the ideas presented here will help you do three important things:

- Learn to listen to your children so they feel heard and understood.

- Use your conversations with your children to teach them and help them gain the confidence to be effective in the world.

- Talk with your kids in a way that creates a relationship that will last forever.

Please don't think of this new list as a set of right answers. Rather, it's a list of ideas I believe can be powerful for your children to hear. For these statements to make a difference in your relationship with your kids, they need to pass a couple of simple tests. Do they resonate with you or make sense in terms of your own experience? Do you think it might make a difference if you put them into your conversations?

I expect you are already using some of these statements. I also expect that some of them won't fit you. But if even one resonates with you—and when used it makes a difference to you and your child—I'll be thrilled.

I'm reminded of some advice from Tim Gallwey: "Don't try to change what you are doing. Just *notice* what you are doing." His point is that awareness is what matters, and if you notice, things will begin to change because noticing allows you to choose in the moment.

> *The range of what we do is limited by what we fail to notice, and because we fail to notice that we fail to notice, there is little we can do to change until we notice how failing to notice shapes our thoughts and deeds.*
> —Daniel Jay Goleman, American psychologist

In the last three chapters, you'll find more information and ideas to challenge you to think differently about the conversations you have within your family:

- **What's Next?**—If you step out into the future and think about the kind of relationship you want to have with your kids, what does that look like? I invite you to create your own list of statements to help you build that relationship.

- **Ideas into Action**—This chapter covers more ideas about creating relationships through listening and conversation. You'll be able to reflect on each chapter and explore processes to help you have family conversations that matter.

■ **Reading Resources**—You'll find books to read to and with your children, arranged by age group, as well as websites that frequently update book lists for all ages. Also included is a list of the resources quoted throughout this book.

It's never too late.

No matter where your relationship is with your children—
whether they're toddlers or teenagers or adults with their
own kids—it's never too late to change the pattern of your
conversations with them, and therefore the character of your
relationship.

One of my favorite change models is simple: Acknowledge
the past pattern. Ask for a fresh start. And then act in a way
that is consistent with the new pattern going forward.

For example, a colleague told me about receiving some
feedback from his spouse that he might consider backing off
a little on how much he hounds the kids about their studies.
Tim decided to change that pattern and had this conversation with his three kids that evening:

"I realize that I've constantly been asking you about
whether or not you have your homework done. I apologize.
I'm going to try very hard not to ask you about it. If your
report cards show you need to change your study habits,
we will talk about it then. Otherwise, I'm going to trust that
you'll do what you need to do. And if I slip and ask you, just
let me know you've got it handled."

Whenever I held my newborn baby in my arms, I used to think that what I said and did to him could have an influence not only on him, but on all whom he met, not only for a day or a month or a year, but for all eternity—a very challenging and exciting thought for a mother.

—Rose Kennedy, mother of President John F. Kennedy

one

I like you.

Piglet sidled up to Pooh from behind.
"Pooh!" he whispered. "Yes, Piglet?"
"Nothing," said Piglet, taking Pooh's paw.
"I just wanted to be sure of you."
—A. A. Milne, English author

...and I like being with you.

You may think this chapter should be titled, "I love you!" In a way, you're right, but you already know you should be telling your kids you love them. You know how important it is, and you probably do this already. Then again, you might be like me: You might be uncomfortable saying *I love you*. You might not have had parents who felt comfortable saying it to you. But those aren't reasons not to say *I love you* to your own children.

I was not raised to be expressive. I don't remember my father ever telling me he loved me, and while my mother often wrote it in her notes, she didn't verbalize it. So naturally, I was not very comfortable telling Jesse and Amy that I loved them. We didn't hug in our family, either, which is one of the gifts of marrying Cindy. Cindy hugs.

I think if you and I are observant and honest with ourselves, we will notice we are not who we would like to be in some situations with our children. And sometimes we need to be confronted in a dramatic way before we really get it. For me, this occurred when Jesse pitched for his high school baseball team. After winning a game, the parents lined up to congratulate Jesse. I lined up last. And then I watched as four or five other fathers walked up and hugged my kid. Somehow, extending my hand and saying "Great game" didn't measure up to who I wanted to be in that moment.

Now, I'm not a fan of beating ourselves up for the past. I think we turned out exactly as we should have turned out given our upbringing and experiences. The question is, who do you want to be going forward?

I like you.

So you know all the reasons to tell your kids you love them. You might wonder, then, why you also need to say *I like you*. Well, this is different from love. Love is unconditional. You love them just because they are your children and it will never change, no matter what happens. Saying *I like who you are as a person* lets your kids know that you admire and respect them. It means you like to be with them. It means you like who they are becoming as they grow up.

Using both *I love you* and *I like you* provides richness and impact. The two expressions are not the same, and the presence of both makes each more compelling. Even more powerful is having these statements become part of the conversational fabric that makes up your relationship.

One caution: It's human to withhold expressions such as *I like you* and *I love you* when you are upset or disappointed with your kids. But that is when it's even more important to include those sentiments in the conversation so that your children know that they—and their relationship with you—are still fine. When you do have a negative exchange or a disciplinary interaction with your kids, it's critical to get back to a normal conversation or interaction shortly after. Children need the reassurance—even though you might be upset about something they've done or not done—that you still like them, you still love them. If they hear this often enough, they'll be able to hold onto that as a rock-solid foundation for moments that might otherwise be challenging.

How do I like you? Let me count the ways…

If you think about it, there are probably fewer than ten things you might want to change about your kids. And there are many things about them that you appreciate, respect, and cherish. In fact, you might try making a list of the qualities or characteristics your kids have or actions they take that you appreciate. Not only will it provide some perspective for the times when they do make mistakes or misbehave, it puts the positive at the forefront of your thinking. And it gives you a starting point for acknowledging and complimenting your child's positive traits and behaviors.

In fact, these are practices I encourage my clients to develop—complimenting and acknowledging the people with whom they work. In the workplace, acknowledgment and appreciation are often missing. People want to contribute. They want to make a difference, and they need to be told when they do. It's not enough to know it themselves; it's important someone they respect notices, too. And that's even more true and essential at home: Your kids need to be recognized when they've done something well.

Compliments. Compliments let someone know that you like something they have said or done. Here are some examples:

You did it! Congratulations!

I like the friends you've made. They're polite and fun to talk to.

You were wonderful in sharing with the younger children.

I appreciate your help with the dishes.

I like being able to count on you.

I like the way you taught your sister how to play the game. That shows you care about her.

That's a great report card. You've been taking your studies seriously.

I'm impressed with how you controlled your temper just now.

Compliments do a couple of things: They provide positive feedback that affirms both the behavior and the child, and they let your child know you are paying attention. Children—and adults, for that matter—like to be noticed, and having someone express approval and thanks for something they've done makes them feel good about themselves.

Acknowledgments. Acknowledgments focus on the qualities and characteristics you see and like in someone. It's what you like about him or her as a person. Writing acknowledgment notes is one of the fundamental skills I include in my training programs. Why? Because people want to know they are valued as individuals—not just for the work they do—and too many people in too many organizations don't receive that kind of feedback. Employees are not sure what their boss or the organization thinks of them. And since the relationship with one's supervisor tends to be the most important relationship at work, acknowledgment is a skill and practice supervisors need to master. It's wonderful for parents to learn, too. Here are some examples for use at home:

I appreciate how kind you are.

I love your spirit. You are such fun to be around.

PAUL AXTELL

You are a fast learner.

I admire your desire to hang in there and keep trying when the team is not winning.

I like your attitude.

I'm impressed you chose to move on instead of lose your temper.

I love how willing you are to try new things.

Remember the play *Pygmalion* or the movies *My Fair Lady* and *Pretty Woman*? They are based, in part, on the idea of creating a new life for someone through the conversational power of acknowledgment. Consider Eliza Doolittle's words to Colonel Pickering in *My Fair Lady:*

> *You see…apart from the things anyone can pick up (the dressing and the proper way of speaking, and so on), the difference between a lady and a flower girl is not how she behaves, but how she is treated. I shall always be a flower girl to Professor Higgins, because he always treats me as a flower girl, and always will; but I know I can be a lady to you, because you always treat me as a lady, and always will.*

In contrast, here is a line from *Pretty Woman:* "People put you down enough, you start to believe it…. The bad stuff is easier to believe." Or consider the senior manager we discussed earlier whose father kept telling her that she was backward when she was young.

The idea is that your words have the power to create. What are you creating for your child with your words? If you see something in your child and you acknowledge it, that characteristic will continue to develop and grow. Whether it's positive or negative, whatever you pay attention to grows. So choose the good things to focus on.

Acknowledgment not only affirms the person being acknowledged, it keeps them from questioning your relationship and their own value. Saying *I like you* and using compliments and acknowledgments are powerful tools for creating and enhancing your relationships, and that's reason enough to express them.

I recommend you occasionally put these affirming comments into written notes. They are the same messages that you might express verbally, but because there are so few handwritten notes these days, the messages carry even more impact. They also don't disappear the way verbal comments can. People tend to keep the notes or cards or letters that are meaningful to them, and the impact can be repeated every time they read them again. That's really powerful reinforcement.

I used to write notes to Jesse and Amy. At one point, Amy told me she really liked the notes I had written to her because, when she got worried about whether I still loved her, she would take out the notes and, in her words, "In an hour I would be fine."

Actions speak louder than words.

This chapter has focused on two things to *say* to your kids. But there are a couple of nonverbal ways to communicate these same messages that are probably even more important than the words.

The first is by paying close attention to your kids when they speak to you. Attention communicates that you care. Being inattentive or multitasking when they are speaking can signal that you don't care or are not interested.

The second way of communicating that you like your kids is simply to spend time with them. Your time with them is a gift. Make space in your busy life to do what they want to do. Read to your kids one at a time. Play video games with them if that is their passion. Hang out in the same room while they do their home-work. Let them help you in the garden. Somehow find some time each and every week for each of your children.

So tell your kids you love them. Often. Tell them you like them and what you like about them. Compliment your children when appropriate. Spend time with them. Listen with attention to what they have to say. And write some notes. Then notice what happens. Sometimes it's pure magic.

Something to think about...

Your kids would like more time with you. How can you make that happen?

What positive things do you tell others about your kids that you haven't shared with them?

I really believe in giving young talent a chance. It has been a personal cause of mine to take talented but inexperienced people and throw them into the deep end, and almost every time they deliver.

—Brad Bird, creator of *The Incredibles*

two

You are a fast
learner.

*Always walk through life
as if you have
something new to learn
and you will.*
—Vernon Howard,
American philosopher

I love that you're so curious!

Let's highlight one of the qualities or characteristics you might choose to acknowledge in your children: their remarkable ability to learn.

For younger children, this is easy because it is so true. Kids are learning machines. Isn't it wonderful how they pay such close attention to everyone and everything around them? A soccer coach once told me that the first move in learning a new skill is to watch someone demonstrate and then try to reproduce or mimic what you just saw. Young children are amazing mimics.

I love watching small children get a new idea. Maybe it's on-off. Or soft-hard. Or open-closed. They start in the kitchen with the cabinets they can reach. Open—close. Open—close. They love the repetition. The same door over and over and over. And then they seem to get it, so they move to the next door. And the next. And then into the bathroom. Kids practice and practice these things until they have them mastered. If only they would hang onto this idea until they get to algebra!

And reading—who hasn't had the experience of reading the same book to a child ten times in one sitting. And the child knows instantly if you try to skip a page! Rather than get bored with the repetition, just stop and admire this little learning machine, fully engaged.

At some point, that perfect learning machine runs into interference—other things get in the way. There are two issues to consider here—one just to notice, the other perhaps to act upon.

The first issue to be aware of is the development of the child's identity or ego. Part of developing identity is the desire to be independent—the need to learn something on one's own, without assistance. On a weekend visit, my son, Jesse, began pushing his daughter, Caroline, on her tricycle, using a pole to push without bending over. Caroline immediately turned and said, "No stick, Daddy! Baby can do it herself." And then she kept looking over her shoulder to check that Daddy wasn't helping.

The other day, I watched a mother take an extra five minutes to allow her daughter to fasten her own seat belt. The mother's patience was the perfect response in that moment. This drive to do things for themselves is a useful trait when learning new things, and we must be willing to accommodate it even if it takes more time. This can be difficult, given how busy we often are. Just notice these moments and respond in a supportive way. I think you'll be pleased with the results.

The second issue is distraction, which gets in the way of children's ability to focus. Maggie Jackson, author of *Distracted*, makes a case for not having a television on in the same room with children younger than three because that is the age at which their learning begins to go deeper. She relates that "two-thirds of the children under six live in homes that keep the television on half or more of the time, an environment linked to attention deficiencies." Recently we noticed our three-year-old granddaughter, Zoe, wasn't in the living room with everyone else. We found her in a bedroom, by herself, untying and tying a ribbon around her teddy bear's neck. We left her alone, and she continued this for twenty minutes, which likely wouldn't have happened in the living room where the television and other distractions were available.

What we want to do is reinforce children's innate ability to learn. In his book *Talent Is Overrated*, author Geoff Colvin argues that if you consider yourself to be a fast learner, you will readily embrace learning new things, experience less frustration, and develop faster. Here are some other good examples of affirming statements about learning:

> *I love how you keep working at something until you get it!*
>
> *Wow, you learned how to do that just by watching!*
>
> *That is exactly how you learn to do something—practice, practice, practice!*
>
> *You get better every time you try.*
>
> *You are so wonderfully persistent—I know you're going to do it!*

I like these statements for some additional reasons. First, they counteract some of the conversations that we *don't* want our children to absorb or accept as true—conversations about being clumsy or not very smart or lazy. Second, life should be viewed as a long-term journey of learning. We never get to a point where we stop learning. In fact, most of us realize that the more we learn, the more we don't know. Third, if we could stay in touch with our amazing capacity to learn, we would try more things and begin to recognize confusion and frustration as a normal part of the process—not an indication that we are slow learners.

A related idea comes from recent child development research. Megan McClelland, a child development specialist at Oregon

State University, suggests it's important to focus on actions rather than characteristics in what you tell your kids. Telling a child that she's smart may sound like a good idea, but it can lead to some unintended results. If the child does something well, then she doesn't see it as an achievement—it's just the way she is. There's no work involved, she's just naturally smart. Then if she doesn't do well at something, she doesn't understand why and doesn't know how to fix it. Her "smarts" have let her down. She might even start to think she's not smart—the opposite of the message you want to get across.

Research has shown that the ability to concentrate, work hard, and persevere are excellent predictors of how well kids will do in school and throughout life, McClelland adds. She suggests saying things like "What a hard worker you are!" Or "I'm really impressed with how you kept trying until you found the answer!" This provides an action the child can take when she doesn't understand something—she can apply herself to the subject by working hard at it.

"In addition to working hard and persevering," McClelland adds, "being able to control emotions (not having a tantrum when you don't get your way) and behavior (being able to stop, think, and *then* act) are incredibly important predictors of both social and academic success—including completing college!"

Something to think about...

Where do you need to stand back and let your child learn on her or his own?

When children are small, what distractions might be getting in the way of learning?

Talking to teens

Should what we say and how we say it change as our children get older? Probably not as much as you might think. In general, speak to your children as adults. The vocabulary you use with small children is naturally simpler, and you might repeat positive statements often to reinforce a message. But the repetition you offer to encourage a young child can come across as controlling or patronizing to a teen. So while it's important to continue to acknowledge and encourage your older children, you'll want to avoid doing it so often that it loses its meaning. And some things wouldn't be as appropriate; telling a teen that he or she is a fast learner simply would not have the same impact.

Here are some phrases that are better options for teens:

I appreciate that you…

You showed real class in how you handled that situation.

I like how you stayed with…

The results reflect the good effort you put into this.

I'm really impressed with how you…

Thanks for talking to me about…

I enjoyed the conversation we had last night about…

Thanks for your insight. You've made me think about this in a new way.

I have total confidence in you—and if you need my help, just ask.

We have to choose to slow down, to actually see the time and space we are in…to truly see people and accept them in their priceless moments.
—Jodi Hills, artist and author

three

Thank you.

*You can't have a perfect day
without doing something for someone
who will never be able to repay you.*
— John Wooden, UCLA
basketball coach

You are so welcome.

Simple courtesies are important in life. They are part of the lost art of interacting with people in a generous, kind, and thoughtful way. In the business world, some say the presence or absence of social skills has a dramatic impact on how people work throughout an organization.

Consider these expressions as a starter set of simple courtesies:

Thank you.

Please.

Would you mind doing something for me?

Do you have a moment?

May I interrupt you for a second?

May I ask you something?

How may I help you?

Does this time still work for you?

Why are these simple conversations often missing both in the workplace and at home? Some of us simply were not raised to express these subtle statements of caring. For most of us, though, I suspect that at home we are just taking our interactions with each other for granted. We tend to pay less attention with our family members than we do with guests. This is good news, because if we simply notice this, we can change our actions dramatically.

For example, when my daughter, Amy, was about nine, she had a friend next door named Jessica who often played at our house. One day, Jessica spilled a drink in the living room. We told her that it was not a problem. We cleaned it up quickly and then told Jessica how much we liked having her around. In fact, Jessica probably felt better about herself after she spilled the drink because of what we said to her!

Now when Amy spilled something, did the conversation go the same way? At that time in my life, probably not. I would likely have responded in a way that would make Amy feel bad.

Why two different approaches to the same event? Well, with Jessica, I was thinking, *Take great care of her—she's a guest.* And with Amy, I was basically taking her and our relationship for granted. It's the reason we often treat guests with more kindness than we do our own loved ones. It's as if I told Amy that she didn't matter to me as much as Jessica did, which was clearly not true.

My point is that when we take our loved ones for granted or stop paying attention to our interactions with them, we not only neglect simple courtesies, but we say things that later we wish we could take back. Or we don't listen or respond in a way that creates connection. Instead, we've put something between us that makes it more difficult to be wonderful with each other.

Saying thank you does much more than express appreciation for what your child does. When you say please or thank you, you communicate that you value your children beyond what is being asked of them. This changes your tone of voice and the way you look when you talk to them. It softens what might otherwise come across as commands or demands. It slows down the conversation so it is more respectful.

Being courteous goes beyond words. I appreciate it when someone entering a building ahead of me waits and holds the door for me. I'm honored when someone offers to buy me coffee. I love it when someone checks to see if I need anything or picks up my plate and takes it to the kitchen. So I say thank you for that kindness. But, more importantly, I say thank you for noticing and for caring.

Some wonderful books that define simple courtesies are worth reviewing and sharing with your children, especially as they get a little older and are venturing on their own to social gatherings in other children's homes. You'll find these books listed by age group on page 178.

These authors have much more to say about the topic than I can include here. But for now, if you simply start treating your interactions with your children a little more thoughtfully, adding a few more simple courtesies, your family will notice.

Cindy has been training me for a number of years to be gracious. Learning to be gracious is a bit like learning algebra or how to drive a car with a clutch or how to cast a fly rod. It takes practice. And it helps to have someone like Cindy to observe and say, "That was gracious…that was not."

That's what you have to do for your children. Your kids look up to you. They watch you closely. When they are small, they don't even mind making mistakes. What a perfect time to teach them tact and grace and respect for others! And what an essential skill set for them to have as they enter a world that needs more kindness and courtesy, more respect and grace.

*Most human beings have an
almost infinite capacity for
taking things for granted.*
— Aldous Huxley, English writer

Something to think about...

Who have you noticed being courteous lately?

Who have you been taking for granted?

Don't take anything for granted.

One of the reasons we forget to use simple courtesies is that, in the moment, we often take the person we're with for granted. This tends to happen most with the people we're around every day.

It's similar to the ability to drive ten miles on a familiar route, make numerous turns, and arrive home and suddenly realize you don't remember making any of those turns! We have this amazing ability to do life on automatic. But we don't want to be on auto-pilot when we're with our kids.

Recently, Cindy visited a friend, Sue, whose grandchildren were with her. Sue commented afterward on how her grandchildren were riveted on Cindy when she conversed with them, which was a natural reaction to Cindy's intention to devote her complete attention to the kids when they were speaking.

If you have the intention to always speak to your children with grace and respect, you will notice when you fall short of that, and noticing creates the opportunity to make a different choice. If your intention is to give them your full attention when they speak to you, you will find the time to listen even when you think you're too busy.

Our lives are not slowing down. Technology allows us to multi-task and keep lots of balls in the air at once. It's often wonderful. There are other times, though, when we would be better off slowing down and remembering the saying: *If it's worth doing at all, it's worth doing right.*

Find the courage to ask questions and to express what you really want. Communicate with others as clearly as you can to avoid misunderstandings, sadness, and drama. With just this one agreement, you can completely transform your life.
—Miguel Angel Ruiz, Mexican author

four

How about we agree to ...

"Just keep walking, Dad ..."

When my kids were in junior high, I occasionally worked with teachers in their school. One evening, Jesse and Amy seemed to be expressing concern about it, so I asked if my working in their school was an issue for them. I also told them that if it was a real concern, they could choose whether I continued to do so. Well, when confronted with the decision, they both decided it was okay for me to continue to work there, but Amy had a request: If we met in the hallway and she was with friends and didn't say hello, my job was to just keep walking. I agreed.

So many big problems can be avoided with a few simple agreements, whether between a manager and employees, between parents and children, or between brothers and sisters. Agreements are the basis for special relationships. They're not hard-and-fast rules that are never broken. Agreements are simply guidelines that are put in place ahead of time to reduce the frequency and severity of problems. You don't need many—just enough to keep predictable, troublesome situations from causing upsets.

In the business world, we talk about agreements between supervisors and the people who work for them or between members of a team. There is no right set of agreements, but consider the value in this set, defined from the employee's viewpoint:

- We will be clear on goals and expectations at all times.

- If you have any concern about my performance or hear anything from anyone else about my performance, you will tell me within a week.

- I have permission to ask you about anything.

- We will agree on how I can reach you if I need answers or direction.

- You promise to be on my side.

What recurring problems in your family might be resolved if you put some agreements in place? You want as few agreements as possible and only ones that truly matter. What agreements are best for you and your children will depend on you, the age of your children, and what matters in your family.

I didn't use the word *agreements* with my children when they were small, but they would recognize the following statement and the fact that it was repeated consistently enough to create an understanding between us:

- If something happens, tell me. You won't get in trouble for what you do. You will disappoint me if you don't tell me.

Then when they were teenagers, we added these agreements:

- I'm going to try not to tell you what to do. If you want my advice, ask for it.

- I'm going to trust you. That means having as few rules as possible. I just request that you think about what the rest of the family needs to know in order not to worry or be upset.

- If you do something that doesn't work in my view, I'm going to tell you. You don't have to explain why you did it. You just have to listen to my view, and then we'll move on.

When Amy told me to keep walking, we added another item to that short list of family agreements.

My friend Ed coaches a traveling soccer team. He says he has only two agreements for the boys:

- Play all out or remove yourself from the game.

- If I speak to you, give me your full attention.

On the other hand, Ed has a four-page set of agreements for the parents because he knows from experience that the same problems will come up each season. Discussing the agreements with parents ahead of time reduces the number of problems he has to deal with and makes them easier to deal with when they do arise.

One of the schools my children went to had two agreements for the students:

- Be nice.

- Do the right thing.

When you think about it, that covers a lot of territory. Of course, kids will be kids, so this didn't mean perfect harmony at all times. But because these agreements were in place, the kids generally knew when they weren't acting in line with that contract.

Cindy and I also have agreements. Some are simple. If she asks me how she looks just before we head out to dinner or a movie, I'm only allowed one answer. This has saved me from my own bluntness more than once. We have a more formal protocol for handling problems when they arise. I picked up this practice from a young man in one of my classes. It requires one person to state the problem clearly while the other listens fully—without resistance or comment or question—then respond in a way that is supportive. Here's how it works:

CINDY: "I have a problem."

PAUL: "Okay, when you are ready to discuss it, I am ready to listen."

CINDY: "I'm ready now."

PAUL: "Okay, tell me about it."

CINDY: "Here's the issue …" *(She continues until she has said it all.)*

PAUL: "Got it." *Or* "Okay." *Or* "What else?" *(Just listens without resistance.)*

CINDY: "That's it. Thanks for listening to me."

PAUL: "And do you have a request?"

CINDY: "No, I just needed to tell you." *Or* "Yes, I request that you…"

PAUL: "I agree." *Or* "How about this …"

It's difficult to bring up and discuss problems. Most of us were not raised to voice complaints or concerns, but we want to change that for our kids, right? This protocol ensures that they will get a supportive response when they do raise an issue. It means you have to listen without resistance until they are finished, find out if they have a request for something to happen, and respond in a way that shows you understand. Then, when you have an issue or problem to raise, you'll be able to ask the same of them—you will have modeled this process so they know what to expect. Very simple. Very powerful. And it's missing in most relationships.

Here are some agreements that parents have shared with me. These are just examples to use as a way to start thinking about what agreements make sense for you and your children.

Ages three to eight

- If you are sharing, one person divides the cake, and the other person gets first choice of the pieces.

- No whining…use your words; ask for what you want.

- If you are having trouble controlling your temper and you need time alone, you can have as much time as you need.

Ages eight to twelve

- The person who is studying gets to determine the noise level in the house.

- If someone made a promise and it hasn't been fulfilled by the time promised, it needs to be done right now.

Ages twelve to eighteen

- If you need to talk, I'll make time for you and won't give you advice unless you ask for it.

- When you are invited to a party, we need all the details of who, when, where, and who to call to confirm arrangements; it's part of our job in keeping you safe.

Ages eighteen and older

- If you won't be home as expected, you will send me a text message.

- If you're out with friends and the driver has been drinking or is otherwise unfit to drive, call us. We will pick you up wherever you are, no questions asked. Your safety is more important to us than anything.

Remember, these aren't rules that won't ever be broken. Your agreements are guidelines that will make it easier to live together. They show your respect for each other's reality, and they give you a place to start the discussion when something goes wrong. As Dr. Susan Newman, author of *The Book of No*, says, "Approach the care of your child as a collaboration, not a dictatorship."

Something to think about...

What agreements would you like to have with your kids?

What agreements would they like to have with you?

Ouch! Oops!

This is from Missy Hughes, a teacher at an inner-city Chicago high school whose class adopted an interesting agreement. This agreement created an acceptable language to use in a situation where the need to appear tough or cool could get in the way of acknowledging feelings or taking responsibility for actions.

"When someone says something that is offensive or hurtful to you or someone else in the room, you say 'Ouch!' Then the person who made the comment responds 'Oops!' to acknowledge that the words were inappropriate.

"It has to do with teaching the power of language and addressing issues and moving on quickly. For example, Craig might not think it is a big deal to say, 'You're so gay for liking to read,' but I do because of the negative connotation he is associating with the word *gay*, and I might have gay students in that room. So by saying 'Ouch,' I simply acknowledge that his comment was offensive or hurtful. When he says 'Oops,' he isn't necessarily apologizing for his beliefs about homosexuality; he is acknowledging and/or apologizing for offending me by his word choice.

"To use another example, when I am frustrated and generalize with a class or student and say things like 'This class is behaving badly,' 'You were all too loud in the hallway,' or 'I am tired of always/never seeing you do *x* behavior,' I will probably get 'Ouched' by a student for making those generalizations. It allows my students to be honest with me about my word choice without being disrespectful. It has also made me choose how I address my class a lot more carefully!"

*The most precious gift we can offer
anyone is our attention.*
—Thich Nhat Hanh, Buddhist monk

five

Tell me more.

But the pauses between the notes—
ah, that is where the art resides!
—Artur Schnabel, Austrian
composer and pianist

Getting kids to talk

In my training programs, I often hear from parents of teenagers who lament the single-word answers they get from their kids. Sometimes it's true of kids as young as ten. It's usually not true of four-year-olds—they rarely offer short answers like *Fine, Okay, Whatever.*

Maybe it's got something to do with becoming a teenager, but I don't really want to believe that. First of all, I know parents who have lots of wonderful conversations with their teens. Second, if we give in to the notion that it's just a teenage thing, then you and I don't have much influence over it, and I'm not willing to accept that. Are you?

Let's look at it from another perspective. Maybe we trained them to give short answers. Maybe it's because we give them short answers when they ask us questions. Or maybe because we said, "Later," but *later* came to be interpreted as, "No, I don't want to hear about it."

Or maybe they eventually learned we don't allow them to take their time in speaking to us. A colleague shared this story about his son, Ellis. When Ellis was about seven, Larry asked Ellis to tell him about part of his day. Ellis replied, "Okay, but you have to promise not to steal my pauses!"

Since conversations often begin with a question, let's take a look at the questions you and I are asking. Consider what most people ask when they come out of the movie theater. If you observe, I think you'll find these are the two most common questions:

Did you like it?

What did you think of it?

These are not powerful questions. They open the door to one-word answers—yes or no—or simple assessment of the movie—good or bad or okay. They don't lead to creative conversation. Consider these alternatives:

Tell me about your favorite parts of the movie.

What does the movie make you think about?

Now consider what you ask of your kids when they come home from school. I'm betting it's: *How was school today?*

Try these instead and see what happens:

Tell me about your day.

Tell me what happened at school today.

What did you learn today?

What did you try today?

Who were you kind to?

What did you struggle with today?

What did you wonder about today?

Tell me what you noticed on the way home from school.

What did you learn that would be useful for me to learn, too?

What fun did you have?

We covered this idea one day in a corporate training class on personal effectiveness. The next day, a young man reported having tried it with his eight-year-old son. This is how the conversation went:

DAD: "What did you learn in school today?"

SON: "In which subject?"

DAD: "In any subject you would like to tell me about."

His son then went through each subject and class and told him what he had learned. The normal thirty-second conversation that usually followed *How was school?* lasted the entire drive home.

As you see, *Tell me more* or *Tell me about* are invitations for a conversation. They're an indication of interest. They're non-directive—the person being asked can take the conversation wherever he or she wants. More importantly, they're *different.* Rita Mae Brown defined insanity as doing the same thing over and over and expecting a different result. That's the point. Asking *How was school?* every day when it has not recently produced a decent conversation is insane.

Begin asking questions like these when kids are young so it becomes a natural part of what you do together. It's true kids can give short answers like *Nothing* to any question, no matter how thoughtful you are. There are times when they simply don't want to talk. You need to respect that by saying, *Okay, and if you feel like telling me something about your day later, I'd love to listen.*

Conversational cautions

If you want your kids to continue to tell you about their lives, there are two critical things to be aware of, especially as they move into their teens and beyond:

- *Be careful about asking too many questions.* This can feel like prying or, worse, an interrogation. If you establish a pattern of asking a lot of questions, kids may gradually share less and less with you.

- *Do not pass on anything they tell you without their permission.* If your kids sense that you will share what they've told you with others, they'll be very careful about what they choose to tell you.

I realize both of these cautions may be difficult to embrace because you are interested in your kids' lives and you love to tell family and friends about what's going on with your children. Still, if you look at the long-term consequences, you might decide to change your approach.

If you want to improve the quality of the conversations you have in life, with your kids or anyone, become more aware of these common mistakes:

- Interrupting before someone's finished speaking.

- Dominating the conversation by speaking more often or longer than appropriate.

- Having the conversation become about you.

- Multitasking instead of being attentive.

- Saying negative things about someone who is not present.

- Overdoing teasing or kidding. In fact, I'm a bit worried about how we raise boys to josh, kid, and tease. This may shut down their willingness to talk about things they need to talk about.

The fine art of listening

One of the most influential articles I've ever read was about listening. The *Utne Reader* reprinted a chapter by Brenda Ueland from her book with Susan Toth, *Strength to Your Sword Arm*. The article was titled "Tell Me More" and described what magical things happen when someone is speaking in the presence of a person who knows how to listen without interruption or without changing the conversation—someone who can listen whole-heartedly and then, when needed, add the supportive request, *Tell me more.* Or the equivalent question, *What else?*

Of course, there are times when good conversation is a back-and-forth affair, even a bit chaotic. But underlying those conversations is the notion of being able to slow down and just listen when listening is what is wanted and needed. So often that's all our kids need—to be heard.

Years ago, I taught a program called "A Special Evening on Listening" for some of my corporate clients and their families. During the session, we did an exercise on listening where the person listening could not say anything at all. It's actually an exercise in devoting your complete attention to the person who is speaking so they truly feel heard. We used topics like these:

What do you like about your house or neighborhood?

What are some of your favorite memories?

When you dream or think about the future, what is it like?

Tell me about your friends and what you like about them.

What do you lie awake at night worrying about?

In the first two rounds, family members split up and worked with people they did not know. My intent was to get everyone comfortable with the listening process before they talked within their own families. Then parents and children had a chance to practice listening to each other. A couple of weeks later, I received an e-mail from Andrea, one of the participants.

> *Dear Paul,*
>
> *Last night my fourteen-year-old daughter, Chelsea, came home and said, "Mom, I need to talk. If you can listen to me the way we learned the other evening, you can save me a three-mile bicycle ride to my friend's house."*
>
> *Thank you,*
>
> *Andrea*

I loved that. What a difference it can make to simply *listen* in a different way. It's a skill that needs to be practiced. A wonderful book called *The Lost Art of Listening* by Michael Nichols makes the point that people typically listen to comprehend or to follow along in a conversation rather than to participate nonverbally in a way that lets the person speaking know you "got" what they said. You may notice hearing the expression, "Got it," in movies from time to time. The earliest reference I recall was in the movie *The Court Jester*, with Danny Kaye:

> *Get it?*
>
> *Got it.*
>
> *Good.*

That's what we're after.

Nichols says that just listening without adding to or changing the conversation is what is important. Reassuring someone isn't listening. Trying to solve the problem isn't listening. Just listening is listening. And when people feel you are interested and paying attention, they actually speak about things that matter to them.

You may have had similar experiences with people who are really good listeners. When you talk with them, they give you the sense that they have all the time in the world for you. They don't ask questions until they feel you have finished your thoughts on the subject. These people make you feel wonderful, and conversations with them are usually uplifting. That's what you want to give your children.

As Nichols writes in *The Lost Art of Listening*: "In the limited time we still preserve for family and friends, conversation is often preempted by soothing and passive distraction. Too tired to talk and listen, we settle instead for the lulling charms of electronic devices that project pictures, make music, or bleep across display screens. Is it this way of life that's made us forget how to listen?... Maybe we lead this kind of life because we're seeking some sort of solace, something to counteract the dimming of the spirit we feel when no one is listening."

Small children will give you countless opportunities to listen to them in a single evening. They often don't even notice when you continue to multitask and only occasionally nod or murmur in their direction. Well, sometimes they do notice they don't have your full attention and say something like "Look at me!"

ROSE IS ROSE © 1995 Pat Brady and Don Wimmer.
Reprinted by permission of Universal Uclick for UFS. All rights reserved.

Start early.

While it's never too late to pay attention to what you say to your kids, it's also never too early. In fact, I love the idea of reading to your kids even before they are born! When your intention is to give your whole attention to your infant, your toddler, your preschooler, and so on, all the way through to adulthood, you create space within which your relationship can grow.

For example, look for opportunities to ask young children to explain things to you. When I visit my grandchildren and we get ready to play a game, I try to ask the youngest person to explain it to me. Once in a while, I need to hold the older kids back as they try to add to or correct the explanation. My preference is to listen and ask questions for clarity. I love listening to a young child explain something for the first time.

In each chapter of this book, you'll find ideas you can use with very young children; in doing so, you set the stage for having great conversations with your kids forever.

Cheryl, my editor, told me about working at home one day when her five-year-old daughter, Cassidy, came into her office several times, wanting something. Cheryl was busy on the computer or on the phone and kept saying, "Just a minute." Cassidy would leave, and Mom just kept working, thinking her daughter had gone back to playing happily in her room. In the middle of one phone call, Cassidy walked in and slipped a piece of paper in front of her mom. It said, "Ar yu evr going to hav tim for me?"

Cheryl immediately said to her client, "I'm sorry, I've got to go!" and finally gave her daughter the focused attention she'd been asking for all along.

Young children don't always need our full attention in order to keep talking. They are busy developing their speaking skills and playing skills. Still, if you want your kids to be speaking to you when they turn ten or twelve or fourteen, I recommend that, when they are little, you stop once each evening, get down at their level, and give them your undivided attention for fifteen minutes. I realize you need to multitask at times. I simply suggest you do it less when your loved ones are speaking to you.

I received this message from one of the participants in a training program:

> *"If you want to change the relationship, you need to change the conversation." Your message in class has stuck with me. I've started sitting down each day with my three-year-old son and asking about his day. I've learned a lot about him already.*

So when kids are small, look for opportunities to give them the experience of being really listened to—of having your complete, whole-face attention.

Then, when they get older, one way of letting your teens know you're interested in what they have to say is, *I'll be ready to listen when you are ready to talk.* Remind them, infrequently, that you will try hard not to give advice or ask too many questions. Then when they do talk, stop what you are doing and listen—really listen, without jumping in with advice or opinions they haven't asked for. Teenagers won't usually give you five or six chances to listen to them every evening. Maybe it's once a week. Be ready.

Look for the signs. When they're hanging around you or making simple one-sentence statements about life, that's an opening.

"I think finding those talkable moments is awesome," Anne, a colleague, wrote to me recently. "With teenagers, this is often late at night, but it's worth losing some sleep to hear your kids' ideas and show them you're interested in their thoughts. We have had some of the best talks late at night when the house is quiet and it feels as if we have all the time in the world."

Sometimes you just need to spend time with your kids when you sense they might need to talk. I used to take Jesse out to play basketball and then just wait until he started talking.

Look for opportunities to hang out with your kids—simply being in the same space with no intention of getting them to talk or even of having a conversation. Go outside and watch them shoot hoops. Sit down and watch them play a video game. Find a book and read in the room where they are studying. If you decide to pay attention to when your kids might be indicating they're ready to talk, you'll be more likely to see the opportunity.

Listening requires entering actively and imaginatively into the other person's situation and trying to understand a frame of reference different from your own.

—S. I. Hayakawa, U.S. Senator

Something to think about...

Who could use a good listening to?

Where do you need a bit more patience, less talking, and less interrupting?

They only tell it once...

When three o'clock comes around it's torture getting out of my office. There are all of these important calls left undone, wonderful projects to do that I can't get started on, money left on the table, and I'm supposed to leave. I never get out by three, but by 3:10, I'm out the door.

I run to my car. I drive like a madman. I get to their school. There's a long line of cars. You've got to wait in line and inch your way to the curb, where the kids get into the car. By the time I get to their school I'm always in the last third of the line. I'm the only man in any of these cars. I mean it's a real education in the values of traditional motherhood, but it's also a challenge, you know—it's that loyalty, that identity challenge. And I'm fuming, I mean out of my ears. I bring my cell phone, my dictating machine, trying to make the most of every moment. I'm just raging in my head about all of the things I have left undone. And then finally I inch to the front of the line, I get to the curb, and I see their faces. I see these little round faces. I open the passenger window. They throw in their bags, and I say, "Anni get in first, and then David get in second," because that's how their seats are. And they never follow my instructions. It's always helter-skelter, bags flying.

And then out come the stories, stories I never used to hear at dinnertime, because I've discovered for myself that generally they only tell it once, and they tell it to whoever is there. Sometimes if you're patient, you can get a repeat. Sometimes even a more embellished version, so all hope is not lost. And quite quickly, I'm amazed at my own transformation from being a raging lunatic to, wow, what another gorgeous source of meaning. It takes about three or four minutes—the smiles, the laughter, the problems.

> - Ronald A. Heifetz, cofounder of the Center for Leadership, John F. Kennedy School of Business, Harvard, *from a 1999 keynote address at the Center for the Advanced Study of Leadership at the Burns Academy of Leadership, University of Maryland*

*The art of reading is in great part that
of acquiring a better understanding of life
from one's encounter with it in a book.*

—André Maurois, French author

six

Let's read.

"Tigger is all right, really," said Pooh lazily.
"Of course he is," said Christopher Robin.
"Everybody is really," said Pooh.
"That's what I think," said Pooh.
"But I don't suppose I'm right," he said.
"Of course you are," said Christopher Robin.
—A. A. Milne, English author

Access to learning, to others, to the world

One of the ideas that has guided me for a long time is the notion of lifelong learning—that learning is something that spans the whole of life, from cradle to grave. In his book *Driven: How to Succeed in Business and in Life*, author Robert Herjavec talks about the need to always be learning and trying to master something new throughout your life. Peter Drucker, author of dozens of business management books, asked people in many different fields: *To what do you attribute your success?* The answers were consistent—they had each learned a series of things from experience, insights that stayed with them throughout their lives and helped lead to their success.

- So how do we instill in our kids a love of learning about life, help them see learning as part of mastering life, and teach them that learning is forever?

- How do we get them to remain curious, to appreciate wonder and the magic of *not* knowing?

- How do we encourage them to be interested in and great with other people?

- How do we teach them to be successful in the world?

I don't have all the answers here, but I do have two—*reading* and *playing*.

The Read-Aloud Handbook:
Ten Lessons of Many

These are just a few of the lessons I learned from Jim Trelease's *The Read-Aloud Handbook*. This is an exciting book in that it provides simple tools for helping your children, at home and in the classroom, to learn to enjoy reading and to become lifelong readers. It will also help you to better evaluate the reading environment in your child's classroom, at the library, and at home.

- There are reliable studies that confirm the importance of reading aloud and of sustained silent reading (SSR).

- As little as fifteen minutes a day in reading aloud to your children can have a significant effect on their becoming lifelong readers.

- When you read aloud to your children, they gain both background knowledge and a richer vocabulary.

- Your child's listening level is not the same as his or her reading level.

- It's important to read aloud to your children individually, as their interests and maturity levels may vary.

- Your children will benefit from your reading aloud to them from the time they are babies up into their teens.

- To help your children become readers, supply books and a book basket in the location where it is most likely to be used, and a bed lamp.

- Far more boys than girls end up in remedial reading; fathers play a key role in encouraging reading through reading for pleasure themselves and reading aloud to their children.

- Studies show children benefit from recreational "lite" reading of series and comic books.

—Elizabeth Kennedy, educator and journalist

Let's read.

"Children ultimately learn to love books because they are sharing [reading] with someone they love," says Professor Barry Zuckerman of the Boston University School of Medicine's Department of Pediatrics. He led a study on the benefits of reading to young children. "You can imagine if someone…came up with a widget that would stimulate all aspects of a two-year-old's development, everyone would want to buy it." Reading does just that and more, Zuckerman concludes.

Reading gives kids access to being effective in life. Reading also teaches kids how to focus and pay attention in a way that's quite different from being drawn in by the dazzle of television. Research shows reading to children early in life stimulates language and social development, which gives them a big head start when they get to school. Kids who are read to have a much larger vocabulary, and that is one of the best predictors of school success.

I'm reminded of a time when I lived in St. Louis, close to Forest Park. Often in the morning I would walk to the St. Louis Bread Company for coffee and a pastry. On several occasions, I saw a father reading to his ten-year-old son from the *Wall Street Journal*. Eventually, I had an opportunity to sit down beside them and ask about what they were reading. Why the *Wall Street Journal*? For several reasons, the father told me. It was something to do together before they went to school and work. He felt it was important that he read at a level just beyond the boy's reach or ability to comprehend. He wanted to create situations where he needed to stop and explain what words meant. He wanted his son to learn that words had different meanings depending on the context or how they were used. And he wanted to expose his son to as much of the world as possible—even if it wasn't through direct experience. I walked away thinking about reading in a whole new way—far beyond the notion that it's something you only do with small children.

A window to the world

Part of what is important for children to learn is to be interested in people, to be curious about the world, and to be comfortable being anywhere in the world. If Cindy and I could take all of our grandchildren around the world or even the United States, we would. If we could interest them in music, dance, opera, art museums, the outdoors—we would. One thing we can do is give them access to all of these things in one way—through books.

Reading provides exposure to the richness of the world. Most people don't have the time or resources or inclination to travel the world with their children. But we can all give them access to books, through which we expand their horizons by reading about different places, people, and ideas.

I'd love my grandkids to be thrilled about how much there is to learn about the world and the people in it, and reading is a way to get at that. When Cindy and I travel, we like to send postcards to the grandchildren. In part, it's because the kids love to get mail. But we also have an idea that each postcard expands their view of the world and where they might visit. It came back to us in a delightful way when Trey, who was six, said he couldn't wait until he could retire so he could travel. As Dr. Seuss said, "Oh, the places you'll go!"

Everyone has a story to tell.

Another great benefit of reading is being introduced, through the pages of books, to so many different people. When you read with your children, you have a wonderful opportunity to go beyond those introductions and look at what makes the characters tick, or ask your kids what about the stories moved them, or wonder what they would do in a similar situation. It's also a good way to introduce the idea that people matter—that, as Winnie the Pooh says, "Everybody's really all right."

It's easy to judge people based on appearance or what others say about them. Kids can grow up to be quick to judge others, scared of strangers, or just uncomfortable meeting new people. And usually what makes a difference is getting to know the other person—learning his or her story. Abraham Lincoln took that notion even further when he said, "I don't like that man. I'm going to have to get to know him."

There are lots of ways to express the idea that people matter—that getting to know them is worthwhile. I like this one from a participant in one of my training programs: "Everyone has a story, and I don't know yours." It was her way to remind herself to be more interested in other people.

And the world is getting smaller. We continually come into contact with people who have different backgrounds, different looks, and different ways of interacting with the world. By reading, we gain exposure to how others see themselves, how they feel about their lives, and how they think about the world we share. Part of this notion that people matter is about seeing the world in a more inclusive way. More importantly, it's about seeing the people down the street as unique and interesting also.

Dorothy in *The Wizard of Oz* said it best as she embarked on her adventure over the rainbow: "Toto, I have a feeling we're not in Kansas anymore!"

And let's play!

If you ask what matters more in life—academics or sports—the answer for me is academics. But when my kids were young and I came home from work at night, the first thing I said to them was, "Let's go play catch." So even though I think academics are more important, what I emphasized was something different.

Still, I don't want to discount the importance of playing with your children. One of the wonderful aspects of sports or reading or other activities is that they give you and your children things to do together forever. Play—whether it's sports, music, theatre, hiking, or even video games—provides tremendous opportunities for learning important life lessons at all ages.

One of my favorite books is *Letters to My Son* by Kent Nerburn, who makes a powerful point about how important it is to deal with the world in a way that leads people to respect you. The flip side, in my view, is dealing with the world in a way that shows your respect for others. I believe both of these life lessons are part of what can be learned through sports. For example, I love it when teams congratulate each other after the game or match is over. The exchanging of soccer jerseys in the World Cup is compelling to me. So is the shaking of hands among contestants after a golf match, or among team members after eliminations in the Stanley Cup. It shows respect for one another, for the other's effort and skill and determination, despite the ultimate loss.

I was raised to win. My father didn't believe in letting kids win—you had to earn it. Looking back, wanting to win played into my being successful in life. It made me practice and prepare. It made me resilient and taught me to learn from losing.

But Cindy is now teaching me to allow my grandchildren to win sometimes. It's a much more nurturing approach, and I like it. This is a situation where we need to keep both things in mind: Winning and people both matter.

If I had a chance to do it over with my own children, I would have put the notion of playing to win into its proper place:

Trying to win matters—and so does having fun.

Be gracious when you lose—and even more so when you win.

When you are gracious in victory, you reveal your best self. You let your opponents know that they matter to you, that you respect them. And when you teach this to your children, or when you teach them to respect and get to know others, you unlock the whole world for them.

So think of your time with your children as a gift—whether reading or playing, listening or talking. It says to your children, *I like you. I like being with you. I enjoy doing things with you. There is no place I would rather be right now than here.* And that, too, is a gift.

Remember then that there is only one important time, and that time is now. The most important one is always the one you are with.
—from *The Three Questions* by Jon J. Muth

Something to think about...

What have your children learned from you about the world so far?

What do you want your kids to know about winning?

A lesson about winning

For whatever reason (shrewd choice of competitions, I suppose), as a child I won a lot. Spelling bees, relay races, scholarships. It was awkward after a while. I remember my mother telling me, "Don't you think you should give someone else a chance to win?"

So, when it was my turn to coach my fifth grade daughter's Olympics of the Mind team, I made a point of making sure we were in it to learn something, have fun, and meet other people. One of the five wonderful girls on the team said to me, "If we promise to have fun, learn something, and meet people, is it okay if we win?" I reiterated my desire for them to enjoy the experience and not to worry too much about the winning part. "Yes, but is it okay if we win?" I looked into their faces; they were hanging on my reply. They wanted my permission to win.

"Yes," I said. "If you want to win, let's win."

They were jubilant (fifth grade girls are good at being jubilant), and I was changed forever. They taught me how to focus on winning without being embarrassed by the ambition to win. They demonstrated hard work, grace, and pride in accomplishment. And they learned something, had fun, met other people, and supported each other throughout middle and high school on a team that just kept winning.

By the way, after the girls won third place at the World Finals, my mother asked, "Isn't it time you let someone else win?" I replied, "No, Mom, they've earned it, and they've shared it with their school."

So one parent's reluctance to win is the counterpoint to many, many stories about parents' over-eagerness to win: pushing hard on their child to excel at sports or at getting into a prestigious college or whatever reflects well on the parent. Both extremes deserve consideration.

—Peg Herring, science writer, Corvallis, Oregon

Making mistakes simply means
you are learning faster.
—Weston H. Agor, American author

seven

We all make mistakes.

Good judgment comes from experience, and often experience comes from bad judgment.
—Rita Mae Brown, American author

...and there are going to be problems.

I remember attending a class on parenting when my kids were in junior high school. One of the conversations that has stayed with me was about problems. It resonated with the entire group of parents when the workshop leader said:

Good kids have problems.

Good parents have problems with their kids.

Life is a series of problems.

There was a sigh of relief in the room as all of us parents got some freedom from thinking that perhaps we weren't good parents or there was something wrong with our kids. What a gift to be reminded that life is a series of problems for everyone.

If I had a chance to raise my kids over, this is an area in which I would do things differently because of what I've learned:

- I would do everything I could to be easy to talk to.

- I'd let them know that problems are normal—good people have lots of problems.

- I would let them know that I make mistakes.

- I'd try to teach them the difference between responsibility and blame.

Being easy and safe to talk to is important for both supervisors and parents. Of course, it's easy to be approachable when things are going well and the conversation is about good news. The time to really pay attention is when a problem occurs. Your reaction to a problem is what determines whether you are safe to talk to, and if you are not, problems may remain hidden rather than come to the surface where they can be resolved.

I remember when a friend had a chance to be with my daughter, Amy, and me. Amy was about five at the time. Afterward my friend told me that she thought Amy was afraid of me. I was astounded. And I started to pay attention. One of the things I noticed was that Amy would lie about things that happened. Looking at this more closely, she only lied when I raised my voice or looked at her in a stern, threatening fashion. When I asked her about things in a calm, supportive way, she always told me what happened. *I* was actually producing the lying. From that point forward, I started spending more time with Amy. I started listening more. I started telling her stories. I worked very hard not to be so scary.

Later on, Amy and Jesse and some neighborhood friends were playing soccer in our basement. I heard a loud crash and immediately knew that my framed picture of a bobcat had taken a direct hit. I hurried to the basement door to see if everyone was okay and overheard this conversation:

> FRIEND: "Let's get out of here before your dad finds out!"
>
> AMY: "No, let's get my dad to help us clean this up and then we can keep playing!"

That's exactly what I had hoped would happen.

Start from a place of trust.

My daughters were thirteen and fifteen when I took the Conversational Skills workshop with Paul Axtell at Oregon State University. One thing that made a huge impression on me was his emphasis on trust. He said, "You have to come from a place of trust. Trust your kids. Don't make them earn it; start there." When I heard that, it was like something exploded in my head. Of course! Doesn't that make sense? What do you gain by coming from anyplace else?

We didn't have rules in our house. We did have expectations, and we made it clear our expectations were based on trust, not distrust. We said explicitly that we trusted our daughters to do the right thing—keep up with their schoolwork, be home at a reasonable hour or call, keep their rooms at least sanitary—and they usually did. Not always, of course. They made mistakes. They did stupid things. But when that happened, we talked about the specific incident, never telling them they had to start over to earn our trust. We "came from a place of trust," and I believe it made a huge difference.

—Alice Sperling, Center for Teaching and Learning
Excellence, Linn-Benton Community College, Oregon

Only use the word *trust* in the positive sense.

Certain words tend to carry more impact than others, more power to hurt. When used negatively, one of those words is *trust*. I understand that sometimes you might be upset or trying to get through to someone, so you use dramatic language like "I can't trust you." It's far better to be specific about what happened and what you want to happen in the future.

> *It doesn't work for me when you don't do what you say you will do.*

> *I need you to respond to my text messages so I know you receive them.*

Trust is a very general expression, and if you want to use it with your kids, this is the best way: *I trust you completely. Both of us will make mistakes, but I will always trust you.*

I make mistakes, too.

Another part of being accessible to your kids when problems arise is a willingness to be vulnerable yourself—to acknowledge that you don't have all the answers, that you make mistakes, and that you are still working on getting better at dealing with various parts of life. For example, I remember one time I came home from work and told Amy that I had lied to my boss.

"Really?" she asked. "What did you say?"

"Well, during a meeting, Bill asked me about how I was coming on a project, and I said I was almost finished when the truth was I hadn't even started."

"Why did you say that?" Amy asked.

"I don't know. It just came out."

"So what happened?"

"Well, my boss didn't say anything else to me in the meeting, and later I went into his office and told him I hadn't started. He said he knew. Which is an important point about lying—it usually doesn't work."

Part of this teachable moment was about taking responsibility. I like the notion of telling your kids that bad things happen—mistakes will be made, things will be broken—and that what's important is to be honest and own up to it when it happens. As I mentioned earlier, I tried to tell my kids they wouldn't get in trouble for what they did, but I would be disappointed if they didn't tell me. I'm not sure that was always how it went, but telling them also reminded me of how I wanted to respond when something did happen.

The bigger message in telling Amy about lying to my boss was that *everyone* makes mistakes—even Dad. When our kids are small, they look up to us. They think we are almost perfect. (I know this doesn't last!) They want to be like us, and they worry about what we think of them when they make mistakes. They worry that we expect them to be perfect.

I believe the challenge of growing up would be easier if your kids knew that good people sometimes make mistakes or sometimes act in ways that are not acceptable. This is not so they have the freedom to be bad; rather, this ensures they don't compound a mistake by beating themselves up for not being perfect or not meeting your expectations, or by thinking you are disappointed in them or don't love them anymore.

Mistakes: the ultimate learning opportunity

It's actually *essential* for kids to make mistakes—it's how they learn. And, as parents, our job is to let them struggle and make mistakes and learn from them rather than jump in to fix things or provide instant answers.

My grandson Adam taught me about learning from mistakes. He was four or five and we were playing the *Mario Brothers* video game. He was doing better than I was, and I asked him how he got so good. He said, "I make Mario die as fast as I can because every time he dies, I learn something new." In that moment, I realized that I was being careful and doing everything I could to keep Mario alive—and I was restricting my own learning by not wanting to make a mistake.

This whole notion of learning by failing is important, especially these days when the pressure to succeed starts early. When kids are learning a new skill, it takes time and practice—and mistakes and failure—before they get good at something. And what we say in those moments of failure is critical.

I was watching a group of eleven- and twelve-year-olds playing football. Because I was photographing my grandson Adam, I kept switching between sides of the field. As a result, I overheard what both sets of coaches said to the players. One coaching staff kept giving the players something to pay attention to on the next play—things like "Get lower than the lineman across from you." The other coaches, perhaps because they knew less about football, could only seek to motivate their kids with things like "Good hit" or "Be aggressive!" While these statements from the coaches were less useful, they probably weren't harmful. Then I heard someone tell the players they were losing because they were cowards. Here was a parent or coach saying something that not only didn't add value but was actually hurtful.

There are four things to focus on here:

- First, you need to create a pattern in your relationship that shows your children it's safe to talk to you about their own mistakes or problems—not only giving them permission to express themselves, but then reacting in a way that's supportive rather than critical or controlling or scary.

- Second, when your children do experience failure or make a mistake, let them know it's perfectly normal. Respond so they feel safe coming to you for help when they need it. Find ways to teach your kids the link between learning and making mistakes. Look for opportunities to reinforce this.

- Third, show them how to take responsibility for their actions or errors in judgment without scolding or blaming.

- Fourth, owning up to your own mistakes helps demonstrate to your children that a mistake isn't the end of the world—you can always work to make something right or do it better next time.

I've missed more than 9,000 shots in my career. I've lost almost 300 games. Twenty-six times, I've been trusted to take the game-winning shot and missed. I've failed over and over and over again in my life. And that is why I succeed.
—Michael Jordan, basketball superstar

I often remind people in my training programs that there are going to be problems, and the correct strategy is to get the problems on the table so you can discuss what will be done to deal with them, both immediately and over the long term. You ask people to bring solutions or ideas, and then you stay with the conversation until you've agreed upon a proper response.

Houston, we've got a problem… I love this line from the movie *Apollo*. If only we'd had our own family version of this! Cindy likes to remind me that sometimes loving someone is not enough to be able to live with them. I think that's her way of saying, "Paul, we have a problem." Her tone of voice is always caring and supportive, but she is also clear we need to talk about something.

Part of being a great team member or family member is being able to acknowledge a problem without blaming anyone or making anyone feel bad. Partly it's your tone of voice; mostly it's your intent to be supportive and to find a way to make things work for everyone. I encourage you and your kids to find your own version of *Houston, we've got a problem*—an expression that makes it easy to voice concerns.

When correcting a child,
the goal is to apply light, not heat.
—President Woodrow Wilson

Teens: If you happen to be reading this...

As a parent, if I could ask you for a couple of things, this is what I would request:

- *Give us a break.* We know we make mistakes. We know we say things we shouldn't. We think we know what it's like to be in your situation, but the truth is, we don't. We do care about you—even when we give you no indication that we do. And we usually have your best interests at heart, although sometimes it's hard to tell.

- *Give us a fresh start.* We want to change, but it can be difficult to change past patterns. If you see us trying, give us the benefit of the doubt. We might never get it exactly right, and it might take awhile, but with your support, we will get there.

In turn, we will certainly look for more opportunities to give you some breaks and fresh starts. You might also tell us where you would like one!

Something to think about...

What mistakes have you made that would be useful to share with your kids?

How do you best teach your kids without making it feel like a scolding?

An apology is the superglue of life.
It can repair just about anything.
—Lynn Johnston, creator of the
comic strip *For Better or For Worse*

eight

I'm sorry.

*The real art of conversation is not only to say
the right thing at the right place but to leave unsaid
the wrong thing at the tempting moment.*
—Lady Dorothy Nevill, English writer

You can learn to say *I'm sorry.*

Jesse and Amy played tennis when they were younger. Watching them practice was a wonderful time for me. It was a sanctuary where I could relax and be alone with myself and still be in proximity to two kids I cherished.

I remember spending countless hours at the Sunset Tennis Center in St. Louis, sitting and watching. Occasionally, however, I would get upset at their performance or lack of effort. And if, when I asked them to tell me what happened, they responded with no answer, I would say something I regretted immediately. I'm sure I used both of these at one time or another:

Do you think we're paying all this money for lessons so you can...?

If you don't start working harder, there will be no more tennis.

You get the idea.

In the beginning, I would never say I was sorry. My mind would tell me they knew I didn't mean it.

Then I got to where I could say it a day or two later.

Then I got to where I could say it an hour or so later.

Then I got to where I could take it back immediately.

Then I got to where I caught myself before I said it.

Some time-honored strategies can keep you from saying something that will later require an apology: Walk around the block. Count to ten. Usually when you react immediately to something that happens in life, you are not as effective as when you wait until you can respond in a way that you like—until you can speak with intention rather than react without thought.

A little time, a new perspective

Sometimes when teaching, I'm confronted with comments that are critical of me or of the workshop I'm leading. When these conversations take place, I've trained myself not to react in the moment, because I don't want to say something I'll later regret.

I've found this useful everywhere in life—on the golf course when I get unsolicited advice, in meetings when people express opinions that aren't grounded in facts, or in any situation when someone says something negative. If I pause a moment, I can usually find a perspective that allows me to respond effectively. For instance, when being criticized in a public forum, I've trained myself to say, "Thank you. I appreciate being told." This acknowledges I've heard the comments without offering an explanation that might appear defensive. I've found that not resisting what has been said allows it to lose its power and sometimes even disappear.

When they're little, it's your tone:

I hope you have one just like yourself someday!

I'm not sure when I said this to Amy. Maybe when she was four or five. She probably didn't understand what the words meant. She didn't need to know. She knew by my tone of voice and demeanor that I wasn't happy with her. And she probably retreated to her room with a variety of thoughts:

Dad is angry.

Dad doesn't love me.

Dad likes Jesse more.

I'm in trouble.

I'm not a good person.

If I could have been in touch with the thoughts she had in her room with her, I surely would have handled this differently. At the very least, I could have apologized.

Can I take it back?

Of course. We all say things out of frustration. It's better if we don't, but we do. The real question is whether what you said is a pattern. If you say something to your children regularly, you can't take it back because they won't believe you. You may actually create a second problem: They can't trust that what you say is what you mean.

Why do we say these things?

I'm not a psychiatrist, so I don't know why. But I can give you some hints that you can consider, and in doing so, you can raise your level of awareness:

- **We are not aware of the consequences or impact of our words.** In the short term, when kids are small, there don't seem to be consequences—they seem to bounce back easily or forget when something else captures their attention. When they are older, you might see that something you've said cuts off communication, at least for a time—and maybe for a lot longer.

- *We take the people we love for granted.* And as with all things we take for granted, we don't treat the words we say to our kids as if they really matter.

- *We are simply following the pattern of how we were raised.* Fine, but we don't have to do this. Even though we saw this behavior from the people who raised us, we can choose to do it differently.

In the end, it doesn't really matter why we say these things. The only thing that matters is noticing that we do and choosing to do it differently. Pioneering American psychiatrist William James once said that you can stop any behavior once your mind decides to stop doing it. I like this a lot because it means there is hope and the possibility that you can be who you want to be as a parent—that you can create the relationship you want with your children.

Something to think about...

Keep in mind, everyone is a little bit scared and a whole lot proud—be gentle out there.

Is there anything that happened recently for which you might need to apologize?

Remember, we all stumble, every one of us.
That's why it's a comfort to go hand in hand.
—Emily Kimbrough, author and journalist

His questions were very good, and if you tried to answer them intelligently, you found yourself saying excellent things that you did not know you knew, and that you had not, in fact, known before. He had "educed" them from you by his questions. His classes were literally "education"—they brought things out of you, they made your mind produce its own explicit ideas…the results were sometimes quite unexpected…
—Thomas Merton, *The Seven Storey Mountain*

nine

What do you think?

There are two lasting bequests we can give our children. One is roots. The other is wings.

—Hodding Carter Jr.,
Pulitzer Prize–winning journalist

Creating resilience

A long time ago, I had the pleasure of doing a workshop for parents and teens with Cathy Pinter, a wonderful woman and psychologist who worked with teenagers in a nonprofit social services agency in St. Louis.

Cathy identified five things that enable teens to be resilient in a world that is at times difficult to navigate. They need to know:

- They are loved.
- They have choices.
- They have influence within the family.
- They add value to the family.
- They are included in family conversations.

We discussed the first in the *I like you* chapter. There are many ways to communicate that you love your kids—verbally and nonverbally. Spending time with them is a gift. Hugging works, as long as you don't embarrass them in front of their friends. Paying attention when they are communicating with you is critical. This chapter looks at the other things kids need for resilience—having choices and influence, knowing their input is valued, and feeling that they're an essential part of the family.

The question that makes all this happen is, *What do you think?* When you ask others for their ideas, thoughts, and opinions in a sincere way, it honors not only who they are, but their ideas as well. The time to get this into the set of questions that make up your family conversational practices is early, when children are small and willing to express themselves. Make this practice part of the fabric of your interactions, and it will be there during the teen years when it is even more critical.

The Merton quote (page 110) reminds me of how I want to lead my classes and how I sometimes want to be in conversations at home. I want to enter the conversation without an answer, allowing the wisdom of the family to emerge. When I'm mindful of this, it has an impact on what comes out of our conversations.

Genuinely asking for someone's thinking does a number of wonderful things:

- It reduces any tendency to dominate or control another person.

- It changes the tone of your voice, which signals to the other person that you really do want his or her input.

- It gives the other person the chance to influence your thinking, which is a real gift for both of you.

Establishing the element of choice

This is one of the more difficult ideas to put into practice. Early on, you can simply give your kids two options from which to choose. I like this. Young children begin to understand that there are usually options in life. Still, it's easy to stray from this because you don't have time or you are sure there is only one acceptable option in a given circumstance.

The point is that the discussion is less about the options and more about the freedom to choose. Kids feel better about themselves when they have the element of choice in their lives. So as long as the option they want to pursue can work, you might consider letting them choose it—even if you think you have a better option in mind.

Let's take the notion of the best conditions for studying. I expect you know the best study environment for your kids. Even if you do, so what? I suggest this may not be a battle you want to take on with your teenagers. Be clear about your expectations on performing in school, then give them some room around when and how they study. Trust them to manage themselves. If they ask for help, or if their performance in school doesn't reflect what you know they can achieve, you can revisit the conversation.

Asking for what you want. A couple of times a year, I encounter a parent telling a small child who is upset, "Use your words. Tell me what you want." I think this is a wonderful practice. In the moment, it helps the parent find out what the child wants or is upset about. Longer term, it establishes a key conversational skill—asking for what you want.

Most of us don't ask.

- We hint.
- We wait for the right time.
- We are careful or indirect.

It took me two years to figure out how to get a whole can of cola on a plane. It finally dawned on me, as I sat with my glass full of ice and a little bit of soda, when the woman next to me asked for a whole can and a glass of water and some cookies. And she got it all!

Your family will simply work better if everyone is encouraged to ask for what they want. That doesn't mean they'll always get it, but at least you will have clarity when they do ask.

On the other hand, being a supportive family member means listening for those hints or indirect comments. Listen to what they say as though it were a direct request. When Cindy passes by my desk and mentions that the light is out in the laundry room, I need to hear that as clearly as if she had said, "Paul, would you please replace the light in the laundry room this afternoon?"

Addressing complaints. This is something I work on all the time, with both managers and employees, but the basic concept is the same at home. Life stops working for all of us at times. We have complaints about what is happening at work or about other members of the family. The key idea here is that behind every complaint is a request. I advise managers to hear people out and then ask them what they want—what is the request at the heart of the issue they're complaining about?

It's the same concept with your kids. If they can clearly state a concern or complaint, then you can begin to look at ways to address the issue. Listening for and working through complaints is part of having a great organization—or a functional family. When people learn they can complain and be heard, the whole relationship changes for the better.

Like being able to ask for what you want in life, handling complaints is a valuable life skill. Helping your kids develop these skills early is wonderful. If they learn this basic strategy of expressing their concerns and then asking for what would resolve those concerns, they will have mastered a vital aspect of dealing with life. Hinting or hoping or whining is not a useful strategy. Speaking out in a straightforward manner and asking for what you want is powerful.

Having influence in the family

In addition to teaching your kids to ask for what they want and addressing complaints in an effective manner, you show your kids they have influence in the family when you use conversational practices like these:

- Ask for their input about dinner, movies, vacation ideas, and so on.

- Listen thoughtfully when they make suggestions, and then act upon them or, when you're not going to act on them, let them know why.

- Let them know that because of what they said or asked, you have changed your thinking.

- Allow them to make a decision about something that matters to them.

- Involve them early in the process of making key family decisions or plans. (See pages 145–146 for more on this process.)

Ask for help.

There is another aspect to the idea of allowing your children to contribute that goes beyond chores and responsibilities—simply asking for their help.

I see chores as assigned duties you expect your child to handle. I see asking for help as a specific request your child could actually decline and, if so, it would be acceptable to you. It's not an expectation. It's simply asking for help.

I have some work to do in the yard. Would you mind giving me a hand for about twenty minutes?

I need to run some errands. Can you ride along and keep me company?

Sometime this week I want to clean the garage. Would you be willing to help me for a couple of hours? Whatever time works for you will probably work for me.

You may need to remind them that they can say no, and when they do, thank them—both for considering your request and for being truthful about not wanting to help at this time.

Sometimes we hint at needing help or think other family members should see that we could use some help and offer. Then if they don't catch the hint or notice, we're disappointed or even upset. Probably better to ask, don't you think?

Adding value to the family

If you are raised on a farm, you know you add value because you have chores that are important to the farm's success. Sometimes city kids don't have chores, or the chores don't seem to matter. Giving kids chores that matter might take some creativity, but it can be done. My daughter, Amy, balanced our checkbook and paid the bills one year when she was about eight years old. Most bills were paid the day they arrived. It worked out fine, except for when Amy looked at my paycheck and asked why she only got five dollars for her allowance.

If you want children to keep their feet on the ground,
put some responsibility on their shoulders.
—Abigail Van Buren, advice columnist

Sometimes we have small views of what an eight-year-old is capable of doing. In some places in the world, eight-year-olds are raising their siblings or finding food for the family. Eight isn't always eight. Kids know they add value to a family when you sit down with them and discuss ways they can contribute.

This is also a place to start early. My grandchildren are always offering to help or just waiting to be asked. The question is, *Am I going to stop and take the extra time to allow them to help?*

It is usually easier and faster to do it without their help, but take a longer perspective here. Perhaps it's not about this moment and activity, but about the process of learning and contributing that you are putting into place for a lifetime.

Participating in family conversations

I've noticed that including employees in conversations about problems is often missing in the workplace. Sometimes managers don't want to burden employees with worry. Or they want to wait until everything is finalized and certain before talking with their folks, leaving no room for employee input. Or it's a difficult conversation, which they would prefer to avoid. For whatever reason, they are not having the conversations that are necessary. This holds true in families, too.

Often we try to protect our kids or shield them from worry, so we don't tell them what we are worried about or what problems we are dealing with. Consider rethinking that. Kids, like employees, would prefer to be included in these conversations, and they can handle the resulting uncertainty if there is a safe place to discuss the problems. Life is often a series of problems. Best they learn that from you along with how to deal with those problems. Talking calmly about the situations that come up makes your child feel more like a fully participating member of the family. So rather than saying, "Oh, don't worry about it," consider something like: "You are right. I am a bit worried about that, and I'm wondering about the best way to deal with it. I would appreciate being able to think this through aloud with you. Would you be willing to listen as I talk about this?"

It's important to start the practice of family conversations early. Many parents include conversations as a part of the evening meal. One favorite is recounting the day's highs and lows—each person in the family shares the best part of the day and the worst part of the day. Everyone else listens and pays attention. In other words, for at least a while at dinner, only one person is speaking and everyone else is just listening.

Starting when your kids are young sets up the family tradition of conversation and trains everyone to speak when asked. Then, as your kids get older, the questions can get deeper and broader. Here are some questions to get some good family conversations started:

What's going on at school (at work)? What are you working on?

What are you looking forward to? This month? This year?

What are you proud of?

What are you anxious or worried about?

What's your favorite memory, toy, or experience?

Talk about a time when you were scared when you were small.

What would make a great summer for you?

What can you tell me about yourself that would make it easier for me to understand you?

What dreams do you have? What's keeping you from making your dreams a reality?

What would you like to learn or try someday?

What do you want to contribute to the family?

What do you really appreciate about others in the family?

There are a lot of resources available for finding questions or topics to enhance your family conversations. A company called Table Topics creates sets of cards with questions and statements to spark discussion—including one for families and one for kids. A series of books called *If… (Questions for the Game of Life)* by Evelyn McFarlane and James Saywell also offers some great conversation starters.

You'll find an extensive discussion of family conversations on pages 138–151.

Consider rotating the responsibility for coming up with the evening question or topic. Your kids will enjoy this!

Sometimes we are friends

It can be rewarding, as a parent, when one of your children becomes better at something than you are. In that moment, the relationship changes in terms of who is the teacher and who is making most of the decisions. With my kids, I remember when

Jesse became much more accomplished at fly-fishing than I was, and when Amy developed an eye for art and architecture. It's about more than the subject; it's the realization that the roles have shifted and you are no longer the teaching person in the relationship. It feels more even, more of a partnership—more like being friends.

You can look for these moments and activities early, and if you look, you'll see them. Especially with computers and the Internet, kids can reach and even go beyond your level of competency pretty early. Ask your kids to teach you how to play *Angry Birds* and watch their faces light up!

This just touches the tip of the iceberg on the subject of raising resilient kids; still, looking for times to authentically ask the question *What do you think?* is a simple, powerful way to begin.

Something to think about...

What have you been worrying about that you could share with your kids?

Who would appreciate being asked to join the conversation?

To say yes, you have to sweat and roll up your sleeves and plunge both hands into life up to the elbows. It is easy to say no.

—Jean Anouilh, French dramatist

ten

Yes.

Children have more need of models
than of critics.
—Carolyn Coats, author

It's too easy to say no.

Remember the original list of mostly negative statements where the number one most common thing kids heard was *no*? Recently, I've begun reading that list in my training sessions, then the next day asking those who are parents what they had noticed the previous evening in their conversations with their kids.

One remarkably simple insight came from a woman who has three children, ages twelve, ten, and six.

> *Last night I was very aware of saying no to my kids. In fact, I said no three times in the first half hour of walking in the door at home. So I started thinking about what exactly my kids were asking for and how I might respond differently than just saying no. Amazingly, I could see that, depending on the conversation, I had options, and instead of no, I responded with:*
>
> > *Yes, we can go to the mall, if everyone can agree upon a time that works.*
> >
> > *Yes, I'll read with you, if we can wait until we finish supper.*
> >
> > *Yes, I'm willing to play a game with you after you finish your homework.*

So here's a mom who caught herself using an automatic *no* and—with that awareness—made the choice to respond differently.

I use this list to make several points about conversation:

- Sometimes certain conversations dominate a relationship.

- It's constructive to notice what you are saying.

- You need to watch for the tendency to have no as your dominant response.

You don't want negative conversations to dominate or to be the overall pattern for your relationships at work—or in how you raise your children at home.

Imagine, for a moment, that you're ten years old, and, already in your short life, you can see that whenever you ask your parents for something, you know what the answer is likely to be. How do you feel if that predictable answer is no? Now compare that with how it feels if the answer is likely to be yes?

No as a response tends to carry a lot of weight. As human beings, we are hard-wired to take things personally, and being told no can leave us feeling rejected—as though someone said no to you as a person as well as saying no to what you asked for.

How would your kids describe your usual response? Are you an "automatic *no*"—or, as someone once called it, "a *no* waiting to happen"? A continual, predictable litany of negative responses can have equally negative consequences to your relationship. By contrast, if you've created a positive, affirming pattern of conversation in the family, then saying no will be acceptable at times.

The point is to begin to pay attention. If you realize that you're about to say no, pause a moment. See if you can come up with a more positive reply. Play with other possibilities, such as:

My first thought is to say no, but let's talk about this and see where we end up.

Here's what it would take for me to say yes to what you're asking.

You have two options … which would you prefer?

Some friends of mine raised their children without saying no to them. Instead, they gave their kids options and choices. This is very useful. Life is about options and choices—you might as well train your children early to examine life in this way.

But what about when the choice is between yes and no? Or when there are no reasonable options? I remain convinced that, at times, *no* is the most effective response, but it needs to be the exception rather than the rule or pattern.

Kids need to learn proper behavior, so saying no to actions that are unacceptable to you is appropriate. *No* is a part of being in the world. When you say no, mean it. See it as the best option, and explain your reasoning to your children. Explaining your response not only shows respect, it helps children develop their own problem-solving and decision-making skills. So rather than saying, "Because I said so," set up the conversation with phrases like "Let me explain my thinking" or "Here's why I don't think it's a good idea." Then provide your reasoning:

No, you can't ride without your seat belt because it's not safe. You might get hurt if I have to stop suddenly.

I plan to fix sandwiches when we get home, so that's why we're not stopping for hamburgers.

No, you can't stay overnight at Mindy's because you have school tomorrow and that's one of our agreements—you need your sleep.

If you start this practice early, your kids will come to understand that when you say no, it's for a good reason—not just because you say no all the time. In relationships, we are concerned about patterns. *No* as a pattern is dispiriting. Being more effective, whether at work or in your family, is about awareness. Like the mother mentioned previously, simply pay attention to the use of *no* in your conversations and, with that awareness, you can more often find your way to *yes*.

When you say yes, keep your word.

In the movie *Hook,* Robin Williams, as an aged Peter Pan, says to his son, "My word is my bond." But as a dad, his track record was terrible, so his son's response was, "Yeah, junk bond!"

What I recommend is that you become very aware of the conversations in which you agree to do something or decline to do something. Be specific about what will be done and when it will be done. If you do, more things will get done. Your kids will be less frustrated with you, and if you are good about keeping your word, they'll have this to say about you:

If my dad says he is going to do something, it's a done deal.

Something to think about...

How many times a day do you say *no*, or *maybe*, or *we'll see*?

What *no* did you say this past week that could have been a *yes*?

Some alternatives to *no*

Not now, but this is when…

One easy thing to do is to be clear about when you are willing to do something if you can't right now. When your kids make requests of you and you don't feel like doing it or don't have time in the moment, it's important to give them a specific time when you would be able or willing to do it. *Let's do it later* or *maybe* can become the equivalent of *no*. So, instead, begin to use statements like these:

> *Not tonight, but I promise we'll have pizza either tomorrow night or Friday.*
>
> *I can't right now, but how about at one o'clock?*

No, but let's talk about it.

If you need to decline or say no to what your kids are asking, it's important to provide an explanation or reason. This gives them access to your thinking and also allows them to see that you are not saying no to them, but to the situation.

You also need to be willing to change your mind if they can find a way to address your concern or reason for declining. It takes a big person to be open to discussing your position, and an even bigger person to change that position!

One's mind, once stretched by a new idea,
never regains its original dimensions.
—Oliver Wendell Holmes, American jurist

What's Next?

If you step out into the future and think about the kind of relationship you want to have with your kids, what does that look like? Will it include talking about things that are of interest and matter to both of you? Will there be spontaneity and openness and trust in the conversations? Will there be kindness and respect? Will you safely be able to say anything to each other?

Once you have the image of that relationship in mind, you can come back to this moment. You can begin to be the person you see in that special relationship—saying the things you want your children to hear.

My hope is that some of the ideas in this book have resonated with you—that you'll begin to notice what you are saying or not saying to your kids, and that you'll see the conversations you have with them in a new light.

Then, as you notice, you can try out some new things to say, some new conversations to have.

Give yourself the freedom to make mistakes. Understand that some things might feel awkward at first. You might get some unexpected reactions, or you might not see a noticeable difference in your relationship right away. You never quite know how a new approach will work, but keep trying.

Create your own new list.

The ten statements in this book provide a starting list that you can modify or add to based on your own experiences, interests, and values. Here are some of the other statements I want my own children and grandchildren to remember hearing from me because of what I believe these words can create in their lives:

I'm proud of you.

I trust you.

You know, you can do it if you want to.

Can you teach me how to do that?

You are special.

I love it when you tell me about your day.

You can plan our day. What would you like to do together?

I'll bet you're proud of what you accomplished.

You worked really hard—that's something I admire about you.

I appreciate it when you notice and include kids who might be feeling left out.

I love it when you smile!

"I don't know" is a good answer.

I'm glad we talked!

Sit down and begin your own list. Take ten minutes and see if you can identify five to seven changes you want to make in your conversations or your relationship. Then set aside ten minutes each week and reflect back on the list and add to it, delete from it, improve it. Do this for six weeks and not only will you have a wonderful working list, but you will forever notice what works and what doesn't work and what is missing in the conversations you have with your kids.

How will you know when you're making progress?

Well, if you are thinking about your relationship, becoming aware of your conversations, and noticing what you're saying to your kids, that is progress!

You might see some differences almost immediately as your children respond to the new things you say or when you ask thoughtful questions and really listen to their answers. Then you might begin to see some of these ideas being returned to you in the conversations your children have with others.

Your words can come back to you.

A participant in a training program sent this note recently:

"One of many things that has stuck in my head from the course I took with you is the affirming statement, 'You are a fast learner.' I've started to use this with my seven-year-old son.

"The other day, I overheard him talking to my wife about some new concepts they needed to review for his homework that night. Aidan said, 'Sure, Mom, I can do that. I'm a fast learner.'"

When Amy was about ten, she came to me complaining that she was bored. I guess I had finally learned that trying to come up with something for her to do was not what she was looking for, so I simply said, "You know, Amy, sometimes life is boring. I'm not going to do anything about it. I'm sure you'll figure out how to handle it." She walked away a bit mystified and not too satisfied. About a week later, Amy was on the phone trying to persuade her friend, Celeste, to come down the street to our house to play. I'm not sure what Celeste said, but I heard Amy reply, "My dad said that life is boring sometimes and we can figure it out."

Eventually, you'll be able to watch your kids raise their own children—your grandchildren—and you'll know that some of those conversations came from your choosing to say something powerful to them when they were kids.

Finally, there is the adage that I never quite understood until I looked at it from the perspective of conversation: If you want to change your children, change their playground and their friends. Said differently, place your child into a different set of conversations.

Perhaps, if we change our conversations with our kids, they will know they are loved and respected and valued for who they are. They will move in the world with confidence. They will be able to handle different kinds of playgrounds and friends. And they will have learned the skills they need to create wonderful relationships wherever they go.

Imagine.

Ideas into Action

Working on family conversations

Creating relationships

The art of reflection

Working on family conversations

At the heart of a wonderful family are fun, vibrant conversations as well as productive conversations. Much of my focus in the corporate sector is on the design of conversations and meetings. Many of the same conversational designs can provide value at home. Be sure to tailor them to fit your family, using language that seems natural to you.

I've included several ideas in this section:

- Ways to keep your family relationships in great shape.
- Processes to help you work through complaints, problems, and decisions.
- Three exercises to work with your kids on the future.
- Individual phrases that can clarify and improve conversations.
- A relationship inventory to bring other things into your awareness.

Spinning your favorite plates

I love the analogy of relationships requiring attention and time to keep them spinning at a high level—a level at which you feel connected and sense the freedom and safety to talk about almost anything. Here are five ways to keep your relationships in great shape.

Hang out together. Spending time together without talking will spin the plates. Just think about what each member of the family would like to do with you, or ask them and then make time for it. Being in the same space is powerful. Board games, cards, hiking, or making dinner together give you a place where conversation that has been beneath the surface might emerge.

Share more. I'm reminded of an e-mail I received from my daughter, Amy. It was concise and to the point: "Dad, you need to share more!" She was right. My personal preference is to be quiet. I'm a good listener, but I tend to be efficient rather than descriptive when I'm speaking. And while I'm a good storyteller, I tend to reserve my stories for when I'm teaching rather than when I'm with my family and friends. Still, relationships need to be two way—not equal, necessarily, but with both parties speaking as well as listening. So just as we notice we're getting short answers from our kids, they notice when we're giving them short answers. So Amy's e-mail reminded me to find something to share when she calls and asks, "How's it going, Dad?"

Listen more. I've given a lot of space in this book to the notion of listening because I think it's the foundational piece in conversation. Carl Rogers, an American psychologist, realized people got better faster and stayed better longer if he just listened to them. A gentleman in one of my classes years ago, who had been a student of Rogers', recalled that "Rogers listened so intently it was as if he were listening even with his shoes!"

Think about being attentive and listening in a way that encourages speaking. Try to listen even with your shoes!

Check in with people. This is a lost art. For whatever reason, we don't ask people about their weekends, trips, or kids as often as we used to. I think this is a missing piece, and it's a simple piece to add to our conversations. And when we ask, we'd better be prepared to listen flat out for four to eight minutes, because that is what it takes to honor the response. A friend who was mentoring a Chinese student received this question, "Why is it that everyone in the United States asks me how I'm doing, and yet no one seems to care when I answer?" You get the idea. Ask your kids about their day and then listen intently.

Find ways to introduce new questions and conversations. It takes courage, but usually if someone in the family asks to discuss a topic, most family members will. If you start the practice of family conversations at the dinner table, this is definitely easier.

Our friends, Chuck and Elizabeth, live in Portland, Oregon. Chuck has a wonderful practice of bringing up a thoughtful question for each and every dinner, whether at his home or in a restaurant. At the beginning of the evening, Chuck lets everyone know what the question will be, then usually around dessert, he asks each person to speak to the question. Memorable conversations are always the result. Once, when my son, Jesse, had a business trip to Portland, he joined us for dinner. At the beginning of the meal, Chuck said, "Jess, I think your dad is a pretty great guy, but I'd like you to tell us what your experience was of having him as a dad when you were growing up." Then we each had a chance to share about our own fathers. I still remember Jesse's response about me: "Even though my dad traveled a lot, I always had the sense that he wasn't very far away."

Dealing with issues that arise

Sometimes we don't address issues at home because we are not sure how to have the conversation. Or our short-term worries about what might happen if we bring up the issue override our longer-term thoughts about what might happen if we don't deal with it.

This is normal. I don't know many people who are comfortable with difficult conversations. But as Cindy says, if we can talk about how we interact and live together, we have an opportunity to be special. She also says we should expect to have issues to discuss because we are two people raised completely differently occupying the same home.

Here are some things to keep in mind that will make starting and having these conversations easier:

- Decide as a family that you are going to bring things up rather than keep silent.

- Ask for permission. This is an important piece of starting the conversation. If you ask for permission to bring up the issue, it changes your tone, and you're less likely to sound confrontational. It's also a signal for the other person to listen respectfully and patiently in the conversation.

- Think about the best time and place to have the conversation.

- Remember that people take things personally, so go gently.

- Remind yourself to be supportive.

- Listen respectfully and give each other the experience of being fully heard.

- Set up the conversation well. Think about what would make the conversation go easier for the other person and for you. These phrases might be useful:

    I appreciate being able to discuss this with you.

    You don't need to respond to this; I feel I do need to say it.

    Please take this in the right way. I want to be helpful.

- Then trust yourself, trust the other person, and trust that the conversation will turn out well if you start it and stay with it.

Three conversational processes to consider

Listen and respond to complaints. This process begins with the person who has the complaint (a situation or behavior that does not work for them) stating and explaining the complaint so everyone is clear. Then that person (owner) asks for what he or she wants that would resolve or address the complaint.

This is what it looks like as a series of steps:

1) *Owner expresses complaint fully.*

2) *Listener just listens, asking questions only for clarity and understanding.*

3) *Once complaint has been expressed and understood, owner makes a specific request (asks for what he or she wants to happen next):* "Please do this for me." *Or* "I just needed to express this. Thanks for listening to me."

4) *Listener accepts the request or makes counteroffers until agreement is reached.*

5) *Owner acknowledges listener:* "Thank you for supporting me."

If you think about it, most of the problems people have with one another are actually complaints. Someone does something that doesn't work for you. If you can express and work through these complaints, then small things can be addressed before they become larger issues.

I'm stupid?

When people are upset, they sometimes use dramatic language to make a point or get attention. It's hard, but you need to look past how people communicate when they are upset. They are doing the best they can in the moment, and at least they are talking!

One time I came home, and when I entered the house, Amy didn't say anything, which isn't like her. This is the exchange that followed:

"Amy, what's going on?"

"Nothing."

"Amy, what's going on?"

"I said, 'Nothing,' Dad!" (You know how they can give you that look!)

She went to her bedroom. I followed and asked one more time.

"Amy, what's going on?"

"I hate you! "

If I'd resisted and said, "Amy you don't hate me," she would have countered with something like, "Let me count the ways!" So I heard what she said, reflected it back, and waited.

"You hate me?"

"Well, you are so stupid!"

"I'm stupid?"

"Well, you do stupid things, Dad."

"Okay, Amy, what did I do?"

"You promised to call me and you didn't."

Now we are at a place where I can begin to repair the damage. I can't handle *hate* or *stupid* because they are dramatic expressions. I can handle that I broke a promise. Not a good thing, but it can be dealt with.

In all complaints, you need to get down to what happened and what would repair the situation. But sometimes you first need to understand that your kids are upset and look past how they express it.

Talk through a problem together. This is different than responding to a complaint. This is more of a coaching process, where one person (owner) asks another (listener) for help thinking through a troubling situation. It also works with developing ideas. This process is powerful for a couple of reasons:

- A problem is always less bothersome when you get it out of your head.
- Explaining what happened to another person helps you gain clarity.

Here are the steps in this process:

1) *Owner says,* "Here's what I'd like to think through."

2) *Listener says,* "Okay, tell me everything about this."

3) *Owner empties out about the circumstances or issue.*

4) *Listener asks:* "What else?" "What else?" "What else?"

5) *Owner responds, if complete:* "I think that's everything."

6) *Listener provides feedback or asks questions:* "This is what occurred to me as I was listening." *Or* "I've got a couple of questions for you about this."

7) *Owner acknowledges the thoughts or answers the questions.*

8) *Listener checks in with owner:* "Okay, now how are you feeling about the problem and what might you do next?"

9) *Owner shares feelings and insights gained from the conversation.*

People tend not to talk about problems since they don't want to worry other members of the family. Or they were raised not to bring certain things up. There is a lot of freedom in being able to say you are wrestling with something and then to discuss it with someone when you are ready to talk about it.

When listening, it's important not to jump into problem solving or giving advice or reassuring until you're asked for your thoughts. Teach your teens how to listen like this; they will be able to support their friends when they need to talk through a problem.

Align on a family decision. Early on, we make most of the decisions for our children, hopefully after asking for their input. As they get older, it's important that they have a sense of truly influencing the decisions. Family vacations might be a typical decision. Sometimes the idea comes from the kids; sometimes you've already made the decision but you still want them to embrace it.

These are the steps in this process for the owner of the idea:

1) "Here's what I'd like to do." *Or* "Here's an idea someone has offered. Let's talk about it until it makes sense to everyone."
2) "What questions do you have about this idea?"
3) "Does everyone see why this might be a good thing to do?"
4) "Is there anything about this idea that keeps you from wanting to do it?"
5) "Is there anything missing that, if it were added, would make things work for you?"
6) "Okay, it sounds as if we've agreed to do this. Is this true for each of you?"

It may strike you that this is not the typical decision process you are accustomed to, where you compare options by examining the pluses and minuses associated with each option. That's useful, but I think this aligning process is more helpful.

Talking about the future

Life feels better when we have things to look forward to and we feel we are making progress. Three processes stand out to help accomplish this:

- Establish three accomplishments for each week.

- Identify twenty-five things you want to achieve or do.

- Map out goals for the next hundred days.

A long time ago I listened to an audiotape series by Earl Nightingale. One of his simplest and most powerful ideas has served me well for over twenty years. On Sunday evening, or at the beginning of the week, identify three things that would give you a sense of fulfillment and accomplishment for the entire week if you completed them. Write them down and place them somewhere you can refer to them frequently. Clearly, life and work will demand that you do many other things during the week. But each time you find some time, return to working on these three things. Fifty-two weeks later, you will have had a remarkable year.

I see two ways you might use Nightingale's idea. First, if you turn this idea toward creating great relationships with your kids, the three things you identify each week might surprise you. Second, what might your four-, six-, or eight-year-old kids come up with as weekly accomplishments?

The next process is an activity I present in every personal effectiveness class I teach. It's a way of getting people thinking about the future they want to work toward. Having a description of the future adds clarity and awareness, which can begin the process of creating and accomplishing the future you want. The exercise is simple:

1) Make a list of twenty-five things you want in life. Whatever comes into your mind is perfect. Don't worry about whether you can do it, or have time for it, or can afford to do it. Just write it down. This is an idea list, not a commitment list.

2) Share the list with others.

I've tried this exercise with a lot of young people, and they all see it as a great way to write down what they want, and they love hearing other kids' lists. Here is what happened for a class participant:

> *The morning of a weekend family gathering, I handed a sheet of paper with the List of Twenty-Five Things exercise to the seventeen family members attending. I asked them to think about what they wanted in their lives, and after dinner everyone shared their lists by reading them aloud. It was a very special evening as all of us, from age five to seventy-two, shared what we wanted in our lives. We learned some new things about each other...our hopes and dreams, what we were thinking about, and who we want to be in this world. We did this exercise as a family two years ago, and my family members are still talking about that special night. This exercise has created more bonding, more commonalities, than anything, and we have started to take action individually and as a family to turn the List of Twenty-Five Things into a reality.*

The list of twenty-five things to do or achieve can be a spring-board to setting goals. Everyday life is pretty busy. Setting some longer-term goals adds a future-oriented focus.

For years, I've wrestled with the best length of time to focus on a set of goals, and I've settled on one hundred days. A year is too long, and a month is too short. One hundred days also works for my coaching clients because we have enough time to tackle some major projects, and we can get our minds around what we need to do each week to work toward completing them.

These are the instructions for arriving at four to six goals:

1) List a goal for each part of your life where you want to make progress.

2) Each goal needs to be doable if you focus for the next hundred days.

3) Each outcome or activity needs to be specific and measurable.

4) List the two or three major pieces required to accomplish each goal.

5) Ask someone to review your progress every week or every two weeks.

I have not tried this exercise with kids, but I expect high school and college students would see a correlation between a hundred days and a term in school. Also, you might think about asking your children to coach you and review your progress each week. They will not forget to ask!

Make things happen. I once counted how many ideas came up during the week for what our family might do the next weekend—eleven! And none of them happened. Why? Simply because we did not stop and finish the conversation by deciding what we would do by when.

One simple idea can make many more things happen:

Let's do thing X by time Y. And, once we agree, let's do everything we can to make it happen.

Of course, other things will come up, but if you put this practice in place, you'll have fewer disappointed expectations. This is a good place to follow Yoda's advice:

> *Do or do not. There is no try.*
> — *The Empire Strikes Back*

Conversational moves to master

Throughout this book, I've emphasized the importance of conversation. From a more practical perspective, here is a list of conversational phrases I recommend that supervisors and managers master because effective conversation requires certain steps. I don't expect all of these to work in your family conversations, and don't get distracted by the way I've phrased these items. Find your own language.

- Thank you. I appreciate being told. *(responding to criticism)*

- Here's what I'm taking away from our conversation. *(expressing value)*

- May I tell you something? *(asking permission to provide feedback)*

- Where are you with this? *(asking for input)*

- While I would have preferred a different approach, I'll fully support this. *(choosing to align with a decision)*

- This is what I appreciate about you. *(acknowledging value)*

- Tell me about… *(checking in with people in order to connect)*

- So, did I answer your question? *(checking for completion)*

- Please say a bit more about what you are asking. *(ensuring you have clarity before answering)*

- I have a request. *(asking for what you want)*

- What is your request? *(responding to a complaint)*

- This is the value I see in what you are suggesting. How might we manage this concern I have? *(responding to an idea)*

- What else? *(encouraging continued speaking)*

- I'm not going to do anything with this. Is that okay? *(avoiding unfulfilled expectations)*

- By when will you do that? *(ensuring a time commitment)*

- What would you like from me in this conversation? *(clarifying outcomes and expectations)*

- I think I'm clear about your idea, and I see it differently. May I tell you? *(disagreeing)*

Creating relationships

Clearly, the focus of this book has been on what to say to your kids. But within that discussion is the idea that our conversations are what create our relationships with one another.

First, let's consider relationships from a number of perspectives:

- Your kids want to have a relationship with you—yes, even when they are teenagers! All you have to do is give them a chance by showing genuine interest in them and making fewer judgments about them.

- Relationships take work. We simply can't take them for granted. Each week we need to explore how we are going to spend time together and how we can stay connected if we can't spend time together.

- Work on appreciating how life is for your kids. Even if you were a teenager once, it doesn't mean you know what it's like to be one now.

- Be responsible for making the relationship work—even if your kids aren't doing their part right now.

- Do everything you can to be less directing, less dominating, less controlling.

- Notice the conversations you are having—delete the ones that do not add value and add others that will.

Work hard to develop trust and respect for each other. For a relationship to flourish and endure between any two people, both must trust and respect each other. We all know this part of any relationship—especially with our children—can be difficult to achieve and harder to keep. The first time you break a promise to your child, the first time your child does something he or she knows is wrong, your trust in the other is challenged.

These are the key practices for keeping their trust:

- Be easy to talk to—especially when problems occur.
- Deal with everyone in life in a great way, in a respectful way—your kids are watching.
- Keep your word when you give it.

Take a relationship inventory.

There are some key questions you can ask yourself to take stock of where you are in your relationship with your children. Ask these questions from your own point of view, but also ask yourself what your kids would say if they were asked the same questions. In fact, you might consider taking this inventory with them—your teenagers, especially. You'll learn a lot about each other in the process.

How do I come across in conversations with my kids?

- What is it like to talk to me?
- What are my kids left with after speaking with me?
- What stops my kids from speaking to me?
- Do I really listen?
- Am I willing to be expressive of my own thoughts and emotions without judgment or blame?

- Is there too much of me in the conversation?

- Do my kids sense that they can challenge my thinking?

- Where would my children say I need to change?

- Do my kids have to be careful around me? About what?

- Am I great to be around?

Are the conversations sufficient to create the kind of relationship I want?

- Do we talk often enough? Am I available to talk when they want to?

- Are we talking about what I want to talk about?

- Am I willing to talk, to say what I'm thinking?

- Am I willing to listen when they need to talk?

- Do the last several conversations we've had reflect the kind of relationship I want?

  - What did we talk about?

  - How did it go?

  - Do we have the freedom to say and ask anything?

Does the relationship provide what I need?

- Do I feel respected and appreciated?

- Do I feel listened to and understood?

- Are we having fun? Can we laugh together?

- Is there a future we are working on together?

- Do I feel supported?
- Is there caring and kindness present?
- Can I ask for what I want and need?

Do they respect me?

- Do they respect the way I deal with the world?
- Do they have any limiting interpretations about me?
- Can I listen to them in a nonjudgmental way?
- Am I clearly on their side? Do they know it?

Do we have any cobwebs in the attic?

- Is there anything we need to discuss?
- Is there anything for which I need to apologize?
- Is there anything that I said I would do and haven't done?
- Do you have any complaints?
- Is there anything you've been wanting to say to me?
- Is there anything you are wondering about?
- Is there anything for which I should acknowledge you?

Over time, without thoughtful care and attention, relationships tend to run down, even our most important ones. Things happen that trigger questions or upsets. Sometimes we might not even know what happened. We just realize the relationship is slightly off. Other times, we know something is not being discussed that needs to be brought into the open, but we don't say anything. In the long run, keeping silent does not make sense.

We also have a tendency to make up stuff about each other out of small things that are said or done. One of my favorite quotes comes from a poem Mary Karr wrote about depression: "Your head is like a bad neighborhood. Don't go there alone."

It's difficult to stop making stuff up, so it is essential to have the permission to bring things up and clear them up as quickly as you can. The questions above can keep things from accumulating in the attic of your mind.

Life rarely runs as smoothly as we'd like. In our minds, we harbor the ideal: seamless days of stress-free work, play, and family—leading to nights of long, uninterrupted sleep. The reality of life is much messier than this ideal, but when we step back, sometimes we see that it is also much richer.
—Mary Beth Danielson, *Mothering* magazine

The art of reflection

Effective people find time for reflection. It's not easy because of the demands of life and the constant pull of distractions. Still, if you want to learn each day from your experiences, the practice of reflection is critical. Reflecting is different than noticing in the moment. Reflection occurs after an experience or at the end of the day. Effective people try to find time for at least forty-five minutes of reflection per day. Sounds impossible, doesn't it?

Try this. When you are in your car alone, don't turn the radio on. Two things might happen. If you have a problem in life, your mind will go to work on the problem. If you have no current problems, your mind will do something creative. This also applies to those times when you go for a run or walk, or hop onto the treadmill. I understand it's easier to get started if you have some great music playing on your iPod. But once you are into the walk, turn off the iPod and give your mind a chance to reflect.

Brain scientists say insights last from five minutes to five hours. Given the pace of our lives, I think it's probably five minutes for most of us. Build in some time for reflection, and you'll not only have more insights, you'll be able to hold on to them.

Our minds also need something to work with—we need to front-end load it with ideas and experiences. With respect to your kids, you have plenty of experiences each and every day. All you need to do is find some time to learn from those daily experiences. Revisiting a few pages in this book each week will help also. The following pages are designed to begin this practice of reflection.

Take some time to reflect on each chapter in this book. Use the questions below to go a little deeper in your understanding of yourself and your conversations in the family. You can do this alone, reflecting and thinking your way through each chapter. Or you might think through the questions with someone else. There is usually another level of clarity and more ideas are available in a conversation between two people. Either way, push yourself to keep asking, "What else?" It's a bit like peeling an onion—with layer upon layer of insights and ideas available to you.

What did you find yourself thinking about as you read the chapter?

What part resonated with your own experience growing up or raising children?

What personal examples come to mind?

What insights have you had:

- *about yourself?*
- *about each of your children?*
- *about your interactions with your kids?*

What do you see that you might try?

I like you.

Reflections and observations from the questions on page 158:

_____

_____

_____

_____

_____

_____

_____

_____

_____

_____

_____

Things to try or look for:

- Begin a list of things I like about my kids.

- What did I notice my kids doing well this week?

-

-

-

-

-

You are a fast learner.

Reflections and observations from the questions on page 158:

_____

_____

_____

_____

_____

_____

_____

_____

_____

_____

_____

Things to try or look for:

- Where might I be a bit more patient while my kids learn?
- How am I a distraction for my kids when they're learning?
-
-
-
-
-

Thank you.

Reflections and observations from the questions on page 158:

_____

_____

_____

_____

_____

_____

_____

_____

_____

_____

_____

_____

Things to try or look for:

- Who have I been taking for granted?

- When do I need to stop multitasking?

- When my kids do one of their regular chores, thank them.

-

-

-

-

How about we agree to…

Reflections and observations from the questions on page 158:

_____

_____

_____

_____

_____

_____

_____

_____

_____

_____

_____

_____

Things to try or look for:

- Where would an agreement make a difference in the family?
- Have a family conversation about agreements.
-
-
-
-
-

Tell me more.

Reflections and observations from the questions on page 158:

_____

_____

_____

_____

_____

_____

_____

_____

_____

_____

_____

_____

Things to try or look for:

- When did I encourage someone to say more today?

- Who would like for me to share more?

-

-

-

-

-

Let's read.

Reflections and observations from the questions on page 158:

_____

_____

_____

_____

_____

_____

_____

_____

_____

_____

Things to try or look for:

- Where might we add a few minutes of reading into the day?

- What different kinds of things might we read aloud?

-

-

-

-

-

We all make mistakes.

Reflections and observations from the questions on page 158:

_____

_____

_____

_____

_____

_____

_____

_____

_____

_____

_____

_____

_____

Things to try or look for:

- What is my typical reaction to problems at home?

- What is my version of counting to ten?

- Who can I give a break to today? Who needs a fresh start?

-

-

-

-

I'm sorry.

Reflections and observations from the questions on page 158:

_____

_____

_____

_____

_____

_____

_____

_____

_____

_____

Things to try or look for:

- What might I need to apologize for this past week?

- Who might it make a difference to if I said, "I'm sorry"?

-

-

-

-

-

What do you think?

Reflections and observations from the questions on page 158:

_____

_____

_____

_____

_____

_____

_____

_____

_____

_____

_____

_____

_____

Things to try or look for:

- When might I authentically ask for input from my kids?

- Where can my kids make real contributions to the family?

-

-

-

-

-

Yes.

Reflections and observations from the questions on page 158:

_____

_____

_____

_____

_____

_____

_____

_____

_____

_____

_____

Things to try or look for:

- What do I say frequently that usually turns out to mean no?

- Where can I say yes to show my trust in my child?

-

-

-

-

-

*In spite of the six thousand manuals on child raising
in the bookstores, child raising is still a dark continent
and no one really knows anything.
You just need a lot of love and luck—
and, of course, courage.*
—Bill Cosby, *Fatherhood*

I'm clear that I don't have the answer to being a successful parent. I do think our intention to be great parents makes a difference. Bill Cosby's words create some space around not having it all figured out—and still having the courage to keep trying. I hope this book sheds a little light on the dark continent.

Reading
Resources

Websites for reading lists

American Library Association

www.ala.org/readinglists

Although generally a site for professional librarians, this offers links to a wide range of reading lists for children and young adults.

Database of Award-Winning Children's Literature

www.dawcl.com

Compiled by librarian Lisa R. Bartle, this site has thousands of books listed. You can search by age group, setting, historical period, language, format, genre, award, and by ethnicity or nationality and gender of the protagonist. You can even look for a key word or phrase.

International Reading Association

www.reading.org/Resources/Booklists.aspx

You'll find annual lists of books chosen by children, young adults, and teachers.

National Education Association

www.nea.org/grants/13026.htm

This link takes you to the "For Parents" section of the NEA's Read Across America program. You'll find book lists, activities, and a lot of good information about reading aloud.

Scholastic

www.scholastic.com

This site offers a wide range of book lists, and you can search for books by age group, type of book, and genre.

Books to read aloud

Several sources contributed to this list: the American Library Association, the National Education Association, and the International Reading Association, among others. It includes classics as well as recent award winners and is by no means an exhaustive list.

Books for babies, toddlers, and preschoolers

Abiyoyo by Pete Seeger

Abuela by Arthur Dorros

Amos and Boris by William Steig

Anno's Counting Book by Mitsumasa Anno

Baboon by Kate Banks

Brown Bear, Brown Bear, What Do You See? by Bill Martin Jr.

Clap Hands by Helen Oxenbury

Come On, Rain! by Karen Hesse

Corduroy by Don Freeman

Eating the Alphabet by Lois Ehlert

Five Little Ducks by Raffi

Flossie and the Fox by Patricia McKissack

Freight Train by Donald Crews

George and Martha by James Marshall

Goodnight Moon by Margaret Wise Brown

Guess How Much I Love You by Sam McBratney

Have You Seen My Duckling? by Nancy Tafuri

Hush! A Thai Lullaby by Minfong Ho

Julius, The Baby of the World by Kevin Henkes

"More More More," Said the Baby by Vera Williams

Mr. Gumpy's Outing by John Burningham

My Very First Mother Goose by Iona Opie

The Little Engine That Could by Watty Piper

The Rainbow Fish by Marcus Pfister

The Relatives Came by Cynthia Rylant

The Runaway Bunny by Margaret Wise Brown

The Snowy Day by Ezra Jack Keats

The Story of Ferdinand by Munro Leaf

The Very Hungry Caterpillar and others by Eric Carle

Where's Spot? by Eric Hill

Books for ages four to eight

Alexander and the Terrible, Horrible, No Good, Very Bad Day by
 Judith Viorst

Amazing Grace by Mary Hoffman

Amelia Bedelia by Peggy Parish

Are You My Mother? by P. D. Eastman

Arthur (Series) by Marc Tolon Brown

Back of the Bus by Aaron Reynolds

Basil of Baker Street by Eve Titus

Caps for Sale by Esphyr Slobodkina

The Cat in the Hat and others by Dr. Seuss

Chicka Chicka Boom Boom by Bill Martin Jr. and John Archambault

Clifford the Big Red Dog by Norman Bridwell

The Complete Tales of Winnie-the-Pooh by A. A. Milne

Curious George by Hans Augusto Rey

The Giving Tree by Shel Silverstein

If You Give a Mouse a Cookie and others by Laura Numeroff

Lilly's Purple Plastic Purse by Kevin Henkes

Lily's Victory Garden by Helen L. Wilbur

The Little Engine That Could by Watty Piper

The Little House by Virginia Lee Burton

Love You Forever and others by Robert Munsch

Math Curse by Jon Scieszka

Mirror Mirror: A Book of Reversible Verse by Marilyn Singer

Miss Brooks Loves Books! (And I Don't) by Barbara Bottner

The Mitten by Jan Brett

The Napping House by Audrey Wood

The Polar Express and others by Chris Van Allsburg

Seed Soil Sun by Cris Peterson

Stellaluna by Janell Cannon

Strega Nona and others by Tomie DePaola

Sylvester and the Magic Pebble by William Steig

The Tale of Peter Rabbit and others by Beatrix Potter

The Three Questions by Jon J. Muth

The Tooth Fairy Meets El Ratón Pérez by René Colato Láinez

The True Story of the Three Little Pigs by Jon Scieszka

The Velveteen Rabbit by Margery Williams

Where the Wild Things Are by Maurice Sendak

Wilfrid Gordon McDonald Partridge by Mem Fox

Books for ages eight to eleven

Bag in the Wind by Ted Kooser

The Buffalo Are Back by Jean Craighead George

Call It Courage by Armstrong Sperry

Charlie and the Chocolate Factory and others by Roald Dahl

Charlotte's Web and others by E. B. White

Dear Mr. Henshaw and others by Beverly Cleary

Freedom Train: The Story of Harriet Tubman by Dorothy Sterling

Harriet the Spy by Louise Fitzhugh

Heidi by Johanna Spyri

Little House on the Prairie by Laura Ingalls Wilder

Mockingbird by Kathryn Erskine

Mr. Popper's Penguins by Richard Atwater and Florence Atwater

Muddy as a Duck Puddle and Other American Similes by Laurie
    Lawlor

Out of My Mind by Sharon M. Draper

The Secret Garden by Frances Hodgson Burnett

Shiloh by Phyllis Reynolds Naylor

Stand Straight, Ella Kate by Kate Klise

Survival at 40 Below by Debbie S. Miller

Tales of a Fourth Grade Nothing and others by Judy Blume

Turtle in Paradise by Jennifer L. Holm

Ubiquitous: Celebrating Nature's Survivors by Joyce Sidman

Walk Two Moons by Sharon Creech

*World War II: Fighting for Freedom, 1939–1945: The Story of the
    Conflict That Changed the World* by Peter Chrisp

Books for ages eleven to fourteen

After Ever After by Jordan Sonnenblick

Anne of Green Gables (Series) by L. M. Montgomery

Are You There, God? It's Me, Margaret and others by Judy Blume

Bamboo People by Mitali Perkins

The BFG and others by Roald Dahl

Bridge to Terabithia by Katherine Paterson

Challenge at Second Base by Matt Christopher

The Chronicles of Narnia (Series) by C. S. Lewis

Forge by Laurie Halse Anderson

The Giver and others by Lois Lowry

Harry Potter (Series) by J. K. Rowling

Hatchet and others by Gary Paulsen

Henry Aaron's Dream by Matt Tavares

Holes by Louis Sachar

Johnny Tremain by Ester Forbes

Island of the Blue Dolphins and others by Scott O'Dell

Lafayette and the American Revolution by Russell Freedman

Little Women by Louisa May Alcott

Maniac Magee by Jerry Spinelli

My Side of the Mountain by Jean Craighead George

Palace Beautiful by Sarah DeFord Williams

The Red Umbrella by Christina Diaz Gonzalez

Redwall (Series) by Brian Jacques

Roll of Thunder, Hear My Cry by Mildred D. Taylor

Sarah, Plain and Tall by Patricia MacLachlan

Shooting Kabul by N. H. Senzai

Stone Fox by John Reynolds Gardiner

Tangerine by Edward Bloor

Tuck Everlasting by Natalie Babbitt

The Wizard of Oz by L. Frank Baum

Books for young adults (ages fourteen and older)

Animal Farm by George Orwell

Anna Karenina by Leo Tolstoy

The Cay by Theodore Taylor

The Dog Who Wouldn't Be and others by Farley Mowat

Frankenstein by Mary Shelley

The Hobbit by J. R. R. Tolkien

The Golden Compass (Trilogy) by Philip Pullman

The Great Gatsby by F. Scott Fitzgerald

How the Garcia Girls Lost Their Accents by Julia Alvarez

I Know Why the Caged Bird Sings by Maya Angelou

Illustrated Man by Ray Bradbury

I Robot (The Robot Series) by Isaac Asimov

Jane Eyre by Charlotte Bronte

Lord of the Flies by William Golding

The Outsiders by S. E. Hinton

A Separate Peace by John Knowles

The Sign of the Beaver by Elizabeth George Speare

Summer of the Monkeys by Wilson Rawls

The Sun Also Rises by Ernest Hemingway

To Kill a Mockingbird by Harper Lee

Where the Red Fern Grows by Wilson Rawls

Woods Runner and others by Gary Paulsen

A Wrinkle in Time by Madeleine L'Engle

Books about manners

For ages two to six
Nobunny's Perfect by Anna Dewdney

Emily's Magic Words: Please, Thank You, and More by Cindy Post
Senning and Peggy Post

For ages four to eight
Cookies: Bite-Size Life Lessons by Amy Krouse Rosenthal

How Do Dinosaurs Go to School? by Jane Yolen

Mind Your Manners, B.B. Wolf by Judy Sierra

For ages nine to twelve
Dude, That's Rude!: Get Some Manners by Pamela Espeland and
Elizabeth Verdick

Emily Post's The Guide to Good Manners for Kids by Cindy Post
Senning, Peggy Post, and Steve Bjorkman

For ages thirteen and older
*Emily Post's Teen Manners: From Malls to Meals to Messaging and
Beyond* by Cindy Post Senning and Peggy Post

*How Rude! The Teenagers' Guide to Good Manners, Proper Behavior,
and Not Grossing People Out* by Alex J. Packer

For parents
*Emily Post's The Gift of Good Manners: A Parent's Guide to Raising
Respectful, Kind, Considerate Children* by Peggy Post and Cindy
Post Senning

Bibliography of authors cited

These authors have contributed to my thinking on what it means to be effective.

Carnegie, Dale. *How to Win Friends and Influence People.* New York: Simon & Schuster, 2009 (reissue edition; originally published in 1937).

Colvin, Geoff. *Talent Is Overrated: What Really Separates World-Class Performers from Everybody Else.* New York: Portfolio Trade, 2010.

Drucker, Peter. "My Life as a Knowledge Worker," *Inc.,* February 1, 1997.

Gallwey, Timothy W. *The Inner Game of Work: Focus, Learning, Pleasure, and Mobility in the Workplace.* New York: Random House, 2001.

Herjavec, Robert. *Driven: How to Succeed in Business and in Life.* New York: HarperCollins, 2010.

Jackson, Maggie. *Distracted: The Erosion of Attention and the Coming Dark Age.* New York: Prometheus, 2009.

Nerburn, Kent. *Letters to My Son: A Father's Wisdom on Manhood, Life, and Love.* 2nd edition. New York: New World Library, 1999.

Nichols, Michael P. *The Lost Art of Listening.* New York: Guilford Press, 1995.

Tannen, Deborah. *You Just Don't Understand: Women and Men in Conversation.* New York: Harper Paperbacks, 2001.

Ueland, Brenda. "Tell Me More," *Utne Reader,* November–December 1992.

About the Author

Paul Axtell provides consulting, coaching, and personal effectiveness training to a wide variety of clients, from Fortune 500 companies and universities to nonprofit organizations and government agencies.

Paul has an engineering degree from South Dakota School of Mines and an MBA from Washington University in St. Louis. He has ten years of manufacturing experience and twenty-five years of experience in corporate consulting. The last fifteen years have been devoted to designing and leading programs to enhance individual and group performance within large organizations.

In addition to interacting with kids, he loves to play golf, create bonsai trees, fly-fish, and read serial-killer books. Paul and his wife, Cindy, live in Minneapolis. Together they have five children and thirteen grandchildren.